ALSO BY JOHN GIERACH

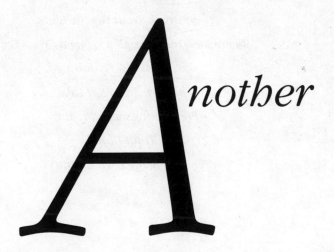

Illustrated by Glenn Wolff

SIMON & SCHUSTER
New York   London   Toronto
Sydney   Tokyo   Singapore

JOHN GIERACH

Lousy Day
in Paradise

SIMON & SCHUSTER
Rockefeller Center
1230 Avenue of the Americas
New York, NY 10020

10 9 8 7 6 5 4 3 2

Library of Congress Cataloging-in-Publication Data

Gierach, John, date.
    Another lousy day in paradise / John Gierach : illustrated by
Glenn Wolff.
        p. cm.
        1. Fly fishing—Anecdotes.   2. Gierach, John, date.
I. Title.
SH456.G54   1996
799.1' 1' 092—dc20   95-53253   CIP
ISBN 0-684-82424-8

The wild geese do not know where they are,
but they are not lost.

—JAMES P. CARSE

CONTENTS

1

Another Lousy Day in Paradise

A long time ago, my old fishing partner A. K. Best and I decided not to count, weigh or measure our fish, or otherwise keep score, so as to avoid the competitiveness that can creep into fly-fishing if you're not careful. Or maybe we didn't actually sit down and decide; maybe it just happened. Anyway, we've been more or less sticking to that for years now, and although it hasn't exactly made saints of either one of us, it's an outlook we like: the idea that success in fishing is something you have to work out for yourself—pretty much without reference to how the guy in the next boat is doing.

Okay, but then after the first day at Anne Marie Camp in Labrador, we broke down and began keeping records of the brook trout we caught and released. We told ourselves the guides were counting and weighing the fish anyway and it's only polite for outsiders to observe the local custom, but I have to say we got into it. And why not? In a confusing world, you have to have the guts to break your own rules.

A.K. and I have always had soft spots for brook trout —because they're pretty, tough in some ways but delicate in others, and because big ones are so rare—and for years we'd talked about fishing for them in Labrador, which is the spiritual heart, if not the exact geographic center, of the brookies' native range.

So on the premise that life is short, I picked up the phone one day, called Doug Schlink at Angler Adventures in Connecticut and asked him where the best brook trout fishing in Labrador was. He said, "Jack and Lorraine Cooper's camp at Anne Marie Lake."

I'd heard of this place and seen the magazine ads saying the brook trout caught there *averaged* $5\frac{1}{2}$ pounds. I can't exactly say I didn't believe that, but, like some other fishermen I'd talked to, I was a little skeptical. I mean, to survive at all in this civilization of ours you have to assume that advertising is a fabric of lies, and this wouldn't have been the first time either fish size or the benefits of toothpaste were overblown in print.

Then again, wonderful things do exist out there in the world, and if you hope to see some of them you can't just sit at home stewing in your own cynicism, so we decided to go anyway. Doug said that, allowing for the normal vicissitudes of fishing, the claims were pretty much true (he has actually fished at most of the places he books trips to, claiming it's part of his job), and as I said to A.K., "So what if they only average *four* pounds? I could live with that, couldn't you?"

So, just to get this out of the way, of the brook trout I kept track of at Anne Marie, my smallest weighed $2\frac{1}{2}$ pounds, my largest went $7\frac{1}{4}$, most were between 5 and 6 and the average weight was, lo and behold, 5.45 pounds: close enough to constitute truth in advertising.

It still seems a little strange to put it in those terms— sort of like saying that, taken together, Charles Dickens, Mark Twain and Edgar Allan Poe average out to 190 pounds of dead writer—but I guess it does make the point. Judging from the world records that have come out of the area, these are probably the biggest brook trout anywhere.

The Minipi watershed is huge and "roadless," as they say —a word I've always liked the sound of. For that matter, most of Labrador itself is roadless: In something like 120,000 square miles there are just two highways, both gravel. Anne Marie Lake is just under 100 miles by float-plane from the small port and military outpost town of Goose Bay, which is a snug little settlement, even if there isn't much in the way of nightlife.

But of course that doesn't matter. Unless you get stranded there by weather (which does happen), it's just the place where you get off the twin-prop Dash-8, drive down to the dock and get on a de Havilland Twin Otter or one of the other planes I really like: the kind that are probably at least as old as I am, but more dependable.

From Goose Bay, Anne Marie Lake lies to the south, in low, rolling hills thickly forested in black spruce, tamarack, birch and such: archetypal sprawling, cool, damp, dense, sweet-smelling, bug-infested north-woods lake country. There are countless lakes, ponds, puddles and sloughs, most unnamed, many of which are connected by flowing channels that most of us would call trout streams but that are referred to locally as "narrows."

The fishing in the Minipi watershed was discovered by Lee Wulff, exploring in his Super Cub back in 1957, and the camp at Anne Marie Lake was established in the early 1960s by Ray Cooper (no relation to the current owners). From the beginning, mostly due to Wulff's prodding, the rule was fly-fishing only, with a limit of one brook trout per fisherman, per trip. Lee said this was the best brook trout fishing in the world and he thought people should see what a place is like when "God manages the fishery"—a statement I take to be more poetic than theological.

Catch and release with a one-fish limit was a pretty futuristic idea back in the early '60s, when carnage was still pretty much the rule at wilderness camps, and they say the guides squawked louder than the clients. But records going back three decades indicate that the fish are about as big now as they ever were. That's a claim not many camps that have been in operation that long can make.

Without getting too sloppy about it, I have to say the fishing here is a testament to the radical idea of doing the right thing in the first place instead of screwing it up and then trying to fix it later. If there's anything wrong with the way all this was handled it's that, unbelievably, you can't find a Wulff Lake or even a Lee's Narrows on the map. On the other hand, you can still fish Howard's Point with the very Howard for whom it was named.

The guides now at the camp are sold on catch-and-release fishing, and they handle the brookies tenderly. Technically, though you *are* allowed to keep that one fish as a trophy—and some anglers still do that—A.K. and I didn't, nor did anyone else in camp that week, but I can't say the temptation wasn't there. I don't know if the guides actually discourage the practice, because it never really came up, but I can say they don't *en*courage it, even when a fish is clearly trophy sized. The upshot has been, in the previous two seasons only eight brook trout have been killed at the camp, and there's evidence that even the head-hunters are mellowing out a little, beginning to wonder what point they're trying to make.

I talked to a guy several years ago who'd been to Anne Marie and had caught a 6 pounder he'd had stuffed. (He carried photos of the mount in his wallet.) Then he went back the following season and got a $7\frac{1}{2}$ pounder. "I really wanted to kill that fish," he said, "but then I thought, What the hell would I do with the little one?"

I will admit that when I landed my $7\frac{1}{4}$ pounder (I mean a $7\frac{1}{4}$*-pound brook trout*, for Christ's sake) I experienced a moment of weakness. The guide was holding the trout in the net. I looked at him; he looked at me and said, "Nice fish, ey?" I said "Yup," and he released it. It was a fairly close call.

Later, over shore lunch, A.K. said, "You're never gonna mount a fish, are you?"

I said, "I don't know. Maybe not."

I've always held off on stuffing a fish because I knew it would have to be a real milestone: a trout so big, so heroically caught and otherwise so perfect that I'd never get another one anything like it. I went to Labrador for fish like that and caught some, but once there I just couldn't get away from the idea that there are not a whole lot of brook trout there, and that if up to eight anglers a week for an eleven- or twelve-week season each kept a big fish, there'd be a real dent in the population after not too many years.

As it is, if you bring five or six of these pigs to the net in a fourteen-hour day, you're doing as well as can be expected, better than most, and you can see that only a greedy shit would want more than that. So sure, it would be fun to have the brook trout of a lifetime hanging on the wall for all your fishing friends to drool over, but you'd have to have no regrets about it, and avoiding regret is getting harder and harder these days.

Don't get me wrong. I haven't become a pacifist or an eco-Nazi, it's just that this is one of those delicate natural balances you always hear about but don't often see in the flesh. There's more than enough food and adequate spawning habitat for the brook trout, but there are also many predators—pike, char, osprey, mink, otters, etc.—to keep their numbers in check and allow the few survivors to grow large. Eliminate or even reduce the predator populations and you might get more brook trout, but they'd be smaller.

To put it in terms of regional history, there was a time when guides killed pike because they ate the brookies; now they release them for the same reason.

It also helps that these brook trout can live as long as ten years, unlike their relatives farther south who rarely make it to even half that age. You'll sometimes hear that these Labrador brookies are a separate race, and for all I know that's true, but a fisheries biologist recently told me it's just that the same species of fish tend to have longer life spans as the growing seasons get shorter. The growing season *is* short in Labrador—it's not that far from the Arctic Circle—but the waters are so rich that the average growth rate for brook trout is still about a pound a year.

So when you get a real big one and you're tempted to

kill it for a mount, you have to think about all that. And if the biological realities don't get to you, you can always remind yourself that for what a good taxidermist would charge you to stuff that fish, you could buy a week on the best spring creek in Montana.

One of the great things about fishing with an old friend is that the same things automatically stick in both your minds, so you can pick up the thread of a ten-hour-old conversation without a lengthy preface. Out on the front porch that evening, looking for northern lights, I said to A.K., "Maybe if it had gone *eight* pounds . . ."

When I got home and some friends asked about the trip, they winced a little at the size of the brook trout I described. I even told it tastefully, starting at a modest, less-than-average 5 pounds and working my way up dramatically to 7-plus. But as the fish got bigger, the eyes of some listeners began to narrow. They probably didn't think I was actually lying, just that I'd gotten excited and had guessed high, as fishermen are known to do.

When I got the snapshots back and showed them around, my friends said okay, but then some doubted that I'd caught most of these hogs on size 16 flies. The only thing they seemed to buy without question was that there weren't a whole lot of fish and that that was as it should be. Any angler who's been around can see the logic in that.

The thing about fishing is, at about the point where it begins to take over your life, it becomes a search for quality, not so much from the spoiled or vain delusion that you deserve it, but because, just this once, it seems like it would be fun to learn for yourself what quality is, instead of accepting someone else's definition.

It turns out that a thing of quality is exactly as it should be. It may or may not be what you hoped for, but if it's not, it's your hopes that were flawed, not reality. In a word, it's appropriate—like the fact that the longest sentence in the English language is in a book called *Confessions of an English Opium Eater* by Thomas De Quincey. Of course. Where else would it be?

And, naturally, the biggest brook trout in the world would be few and far between, wouldn't they?

So most of our days in Labrador were spent hunting fish: out in the morning after breakfast, lunch on a sandbar somewhere, back to the camp for supper and then back out on the water until about ten in the evening, later if things were really cooking.

There's a lot of water here, but there are only a relative handful of more or less dependable spots where the brook trout are known to congregate at certain times of year. On any given day you tour a few of those places off in one direction or another, sometimes hitting the same ones at intervals of a couple of hours because, you know, something could have changed—a hatch could have come on.

Now and then, if things were slow, we'd end up blind casting with streamers at the inlets and outlets of narrows where, if fish were there and hungry, there were more or less obvious places for them to be holding. But mostly we cruised in a flat-sterned canoe with an 8-horse outboard, looking for rising fish.

If the trout were working, they were usually around some kind of structure—a rocky point or a bed of lily pads. The guide would roar up in the boat, cutting the motor far out to keep the wake down, and then quietly switching to a paddle. Then we'd all watch for a while, usually without conversation. If fish were rising, boiling, tailing or otherwise showing themselves, we'd cast to them. If not, we'd watch for a while longer, then crank up the outboard and try another spot.

Most days there were several hours of furious fishing and as many more hours of cruising in the canoe with time to relax and look around. This is lovely, green, silent country, and you're far enough into it that you won't meet anyone you didn't have breakfast with that morning. Sometimes I'd sit back and think, I might come to a place like this just for the hell of it, even if there weren't huge brook trout.

That's crap, of course; it's just that when I'm in wild country far from home I tend to feel calmer and more grateful to be alive than I really am. Maybe that's why I do this.

You fall into a routine at a fishing camp, and at a *good* camp you almost begin to feel at home. I liked this place. The four-bedroom cabin, with woodstove, that serves as a lodge is old, clean, comfortable and funky. There are no vaulted ceilings, no two-story picture windows, no fabulous collections of game mounts. (What looks at first like a big, stuffed brookie is actually a painted wood carving.) This is a by-God cabin in the north woods where fishermen stay, built out on an open point to catch the breeze off the lake. If some mosquitos get in at night and there aren't enough bats in the loft to eat them all, those are the breaks.

And the people have that firm grasp on reality I always envy in those who make a living in the real world, whether they guide fishermen or grow corn. Rule one is, Well, I won't get it done sittin' here drinking coffee. Rule two is, The best you can do is the best you can do, so don't panic.

•

They say if you're going to fish for brook trout in Labrador you should bring lots of dry flies and nymphs in lots of different sizes because there are many hatches and they're mostly uncatalogued. A fly-tying kit would be handy, but it would also be a clumsy piece of luggage, considering that the round trip from Denver takes ten separate flights over four days.

The guides are pretty casual about fly patterns—much more so than some of the clients—and that's refreshing. Fly-fishing does get way too scientific at times, although I guess that still beats the phony-macho, pulp-magazine approach I grew up with. Back in the 1950s, this story would have been called, "I Fought Labrador's Killer Trout and Lived!"

It's also a good idea to have some streamers—Muddlers and Mickey Finns are favorites—and some #2 deer-hair lemmings. (Okay, if you're not an absolute purist, a mouse pattern or even a bass bug will do.) We didn't see any lemming action, but I'm told that in years when these little critters' populations are high, the brookies feed on them ravenously. It's best to have a fair number of streamers and mice because, unless you're in the habit of fishing wire leaders for brook trout, you'll lose some of your big flies to pike.

The guides say the hatches of the really big bugs— stoneflies, mayflies and caddis all up to size 2 and 4—are glorious but unpredictable; that during some hatches you'll catch big landlocked arctic char on dry flies; that a snowshoe hare is called an *ookalik;* that Sasquatches can sometimes be heard howling in the night and so on. They say a lot of things in the course of a week's fishing and, since these guides have been there a long time and seem to know what they're talking about, you listen. Eventually you get a faint but larger picture, even though as a tourist sport you know you'll only ever see thin slices of the local reality.

Friends back home have asked me if the brook trout up there were selective. That's the third question a fisherman asks, after "How many?" and "How big?" In translation it means, "Are they easy?" because, after all, brook trout have the *reputation* for being easy.

The answer, as always, is yes and no. Mostly we tried to match the shape, size, color and action of the bugs the fish were feeding on because that's just how we fish, but the accepted wisdom is, these fish are huge and wild, but they're still brook trout with a brook trout's inherent goofiness. So if what should work, doesn't, you try something else. Hell, try a lemming.

Looking back on it now, most of the trip runs together, as most trips do, while some parts stand out clearly, self-contained.

We saw a few long, lazy multiple hatches lasting half a day or more, stalked a few solitary risers, and one night after dark we sound-fished to huge brookies rising to a spinner fall on a silent, glassy pond between two narrows.

We found a few fish that were very picky (one refused three or four little mayfly dun patterns and finally took an emerger) and a few that would eat a #8 Royal Wulff when there was nothing like a Royal Wulff hatch on the water, or chase a dragged Muddler through a sedate hatch of small mayflies.

One afternoon, a long boat ride and a long portage from camp, we were casting streamers in a lonely stretch of running water. I'd been standing in one spot for almost an hour, running one streamer and then another along a likely looking far bank without a strike, while A.K., fifty yards downstream, had landed two brookies weighing something like 5½ and 6 pounds.

Finally I broke down and yelled, "Okay, what the hell are you using?"

He said, "Size 4 Muddler, of course," as if only an idiot would have failed to deduce the obvious by now.

So I changed flies.

Now, you know how when you've just tied on a new fly and you're standing there with the tippet in your hand and the rod under your arm, you'll just toss the fly on the water at your feet before you start casting? Well, I did that, and a 5-pound brook trout came out from under the rock I was standing on and ate it.

All I could do was pay line out through my fingers until I could get hold of the rod at the ferrule, hand-over-hand my way down to the grip and get the fish on the reel. Once I got things under control and began playing the fish in the conventional manner, I glanced downstream. A.K. was laughing so hard he had to lean on a big boulder to keep from falling in the river. Ray, the guide, was polite enough to just shake his head and grin.

Too bad. I was hoping they hadn't seen it. I did land the fish, though, and I think I handled the whole thing pretty damned well, all things considered.

The weather that week was mostly warm and bright, but we were also treated to a couple days of that maritime rain, wind and cold you can get in the neighborhood of the North Atlantic.

At around ten-thirty at night on the second day of the storm, we were heading back to camp and we had to cross a long, exposed stretch of lake that was boiling up into

2-foot whitecaps. We were in a 16-foot canoe with an 8-horse outboard.

If I'd been driving the boat, we'd have been slapped silly and drenched within half a mile, if not outright swamped and drowned, but our guide for that day—Howard, of Howard's Point fame—slowly rode the swells, gunning the motor gently to slide from one wave to the next, rocking the canoe no more than you'd rock a cradle. There was too much wind and engine noise to yell over, but A.K. turned around in the bow, gave me an amazed look and nodded at Howard by way of saying, "Hell of a boatman." I grinned and nodded back, "Yup, hell of a boatman."

It had been an uncomfortable day of fishing, though somewhat short of actual misery. We'd been wet and chilly since half an hour after breakfast, the coffee at lunch was good and hot, but the sandwiches were soggy. The wind had been biting, but when it calmed to that eerie northwoods silence, the mosquitos materialized, sounding like the whining of a thousand distant dentist's drills. We'd caught some fish. Big ones.

I remember being cold and generally beat up coming back across the lake that night. I wasn't hypothermic, but I was chattering a little, my fingers were numb, and bug bites itched where there was still some feeling. Maybe a mile across the lake, we could see the porch light at the cabin —the only electric light for a hundred miles.

I remember feeling good. Not like Superman or anything, it's just that I was wet and cold in a small canoe on a big lake in a storm a hundred miles from anywhere and I didn't feel fragile or even especially tired. All in all, it was just another lousy day in paradise.

•

So we did well, but there were fish we couldn't catch and some we hooked but couldn't land, which is as it should be. Most days we fished at a pretty leisurely pace, what with the long canoe rides and all, but between the high drama of trying to hook trophy fish and the elation of landing a few, I found it was possible to become emotionally exhausted. By the end of a day I was tired enough that even A.K.'s god-awful snoring didn't keep me awake.

It was glorious fishing, and in six and a half days of it I think I managed not to get too spoiled. Okay, one time I did refer to a $3\frac{1}{2}$-pound brookie as "a little one," but A.K. gave me one of his schoolteacher scowls, and I said, "Yeah, right, what the hell am I saying?"

A week of cosmic fishing never quite seems like enough at the time, but it probably is. I mean, just before you actually start to get used to it, the floatplane comes to take you back to civilization. One morning you're in camp, drinking strong coffee and joking with Helen, the cook. That evening you're in a bar in Halifax, trying to ignore the canned music. You've already made plans to book another week the following year and the conversation has wound down to ten minutes of silence. Then someone says, "Jeez, I didn't think they made brook trout that big!" It's probably best that you left before the newness of it started to wear off.

I guess I should say, the floatplane *usually* comes to take you back. Operations like this often have better on-time records than the major airlines, but this is bush flying, and delays aren't unheard of.

One of the guides told me about a guy who, on what he thought was his last night in camp, drank all his whiskey and gave away all his cigars. Then the weather turned bad and he was stuck there for two more days. To his credit, he didn't ask for his cigars back, but you could tell he wanted to.

And there was this entry in the camp log: "Last day, weather socked in so plane can't come to take us out. Only three fishermen injured in scramble to get back on the water."

We never got around to fishing for the char or pike (both respectable game fish, just not quite as sexy as trophy brook trout), but I did get one northern by accident. We'd anchored the canoe at the head of a narrows, and I was playing a nice brook trout. It was going well, and I nearly had him to the boat when the line thumped once and went dead. This was a spot where I'd already lost several big fish to the jumbled boulders on the bottom, getting back nothing but a frayed leader, so I said, "Shit, I think he's got me in the rocks."

Our Guide, Al, peered over the gunnel and said, "No, a poik's got 'im."

The light was poor, but I could just make it out down there: my big brook trout with a long green thing that could only be a northern pike hanging off it. I carefully hauled the brookie toward the surface, and the pike was either unwilling or unable to let go, so Al netted them together.

It was a mess, but we got them untangled and released both fish. The brookie was stunned, but he wasn't too badly injured, considering. After a little resuscitation, he swam off strongly and I like to think he survived. The trout weighed 6 pounds, the pike, $9\frac{1}{2}$ and—since we were counting such things on this trip—I guess I'll always think of it as $15\frac{1}{2}$ pounds of fish on a #16 dry fly.

On our last night in camp, I was filling out the log book and, bowing to local custom, I recorded that in six and a half days, five fishermen had landed and released fifty brook trout with a total weight of 253 pounds and an average weight of 5.1 pounds. My pike was the only one caught (if you can call it that), and I asked A.K. how he thought I should enter it.

He said, "I guess you'll have to say you got it on live bait."

2

Rock Bass

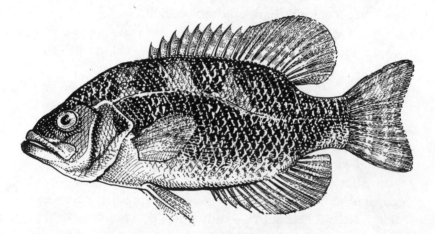

A couple of seasons ago, a fisheries biologist with the Colorado Division of Wildlife asked me if I could get him some rock bass. It just came up by accident in conversation. He was asking me about some of the warm-water ponds I fished—out of professional curiosity, since he's in charge of managing most of them, and also out of the common (though often mistaken) idea that fishing writers know more about this stuff than regular old fishermen. In the course of things, I happened to mention that, in addition to the largemouth bass and the various kinds of sunfish I was getting, I sometimes caught rock bass.

He perked up at that, said he'd been trying to get a few rock bass as specimens, but in all the netting and shocking surveys he'd done, he hadn't been able to turn any up, even though he knew there were some around.

The rock bass is a pretty common sunfish, as sunfish go, but there are so few of them in Colorado they're not even listed in the fishing regulations, and not every fisherman recognizes them. They're a little fatter and more robust than most of the sunfishes, but otherwise they just look like a chunky, dark-colored bluegill.

"If I gave you a jug of Formalin, do you suppose you could get me a few?" he asked. "They wouldn't have to be big."

I said sure, I could do that. The guy had helped me out with tips and information a few times, and I guess I was flattered that he couldn't get a couple of little rock bass with all his scientific collection techniques, but he thought I could with a fly rod.

After all, as an official biologist for a state agency, this guy had some serious resources at his disposal, not to mention a federal permit that—although I don't remember the exact wording—allowed him to catch, trap; snare, shoot or otherwise take any species by any means at any time, period, no exceptions.

He showed it to me once. Considering that it was the cosmic fishing and hunting license, it was a small, deceptively modest-looking document.

I said, "I know a couple of guys who could use one of those."

"I'll just bet you do," he replied.

So I picked up the 5-gallon plastic pickle jar of Formalin—a solution of formaldehyde, methanol and water used to store specimens temporarily—and got the short lecture on how to use it.

"Now you want to put them in here alive," he said, "so they pump the stuff through their systems before they die, but you probably don't want to *watch* that. And don't get any of it on you."

I did know of a couple of ponds that had some rock bass, and I even knew where in the ponds to look, not that that was much of a trick. For reasons of their own, these fish like riprap banks—stone rubble and large rocks—hence their name.

This was no big deal—just a small, return favor for a nice guy—but, driving home with that jug of gunk in the bed of the pickup, I really enjoyed being someone you could ask to locate and identify a certain obscure little sunfish. When it comes right down to it, I think that's the secret ambition of every fly fisher: just to be someone who knows the territory.

When I moved out here to the Rocky Mountains, almost exactly a quarter of a century ago now, I didn't do it entirely for the fly-fishing, although that was part of it. A larger part, I think, was the idea of learning the place and making myself at home here. It wasn't until later that I fully realized how much fly-fishing had to do with that.

Sure, I could have stayed in the Midwest and learned to be at home *there*, but I think I saw things in the heartland going in the wrong direction, so I came out West to start over. After all, that's what dissatisfied Americans have been doing for the last two hundred years, never mind that if you come West now you'll meet the eastward migration of Californians who've sold their surfboards and are now trying to retrace their steps.

I did want to learn how to fly fish, but there were other considerations—most of which I've all but forgotten by now—and because of them I rattled around Colorado for a while, working odd jobs, living in odd places with odd people, and finally ended up on the outskirts of a small, foothills town on the East Slope, a stone's throw from what, in the grand scheme of things, you'd have to describe as a fair to middling little trout creek.

Besides the creek, there's a lot of other fishing nearby, and if none of it is downright fabulous, there's at least a good variety.

And this is also a great jumping-off place. Within a day's drive of here are maybe a quarter of the best trout streams and rivers in the West. Add a second day on the road and you're probably in range of over half. More water than a guy could adequately fish in a lifetime.

Hell, I still haven't even fished all of the 300-some miles of the nearest local drainage—although I'm still working on it—and even after all this time, I could probably make a longer list of places in the region I'd like to fish than of places I *have* fished. But I still feel like I know the area pretty well.

For instance, it took me a few trips to get my friend his elusive rock bass, but I did finally manage it. He'd said all he wanted were little ones and that, actually, little ones were all he'd ever seen. So I pickled five dinks and one nice big one, just because I thought he'd appreciate that. Under "location" on the form he gave me, I wrote "Nameless pond in Boulder County." To his credit, he never asked me to be more specific.

I've lived in the same old house since 1977, but of course it's not quite as sleepy and quiet here as it was when I moved in eighteen years ago. That little town down the road has grown out to meet me, and although I'm officially still in the county, the town limit now lies up against my property line, which strikes me as a little too close for comfort. They keep asking me to annex and I keep saying, "If I'd wanted to live in town, I'd have bought a house in town in the first place."

Okay, that's a technicality, but it seems important because where you live in relation to a town is a lot like where you place yourself in society in general. That is, you don't have to be completely outside of it, but you should stay close enough to the edge to be able to see out.

If a handful of people have their way, the town will grow more and faster than it has already, against the wishes of almost everyone who lives here, but then it's always possible that certain greedy developers and politicians *won't* have their way. That does happen, you know.

Since I've lived here I've been involved in an effort that killed one development, another that just recently mounted a referendum and reversed a 40-acre annexation for a monster housing project, and also an ongoing movement to put a little water back into the creek for the trout, although the jury is still out on that last one.

Not long ago a town official pointed out that I was, after all, just a county resident and accused me of being an "outside agitator" in the town's affairs, an epithet I haven't heard since the 1960s. Luckily I had the presence of mind to say, "Right. What's your point?"

Any grass-roots political effort is so easily derailed by money, influence, arrogance and bureaucracy on the opposing side and by laziness, rage, egotism and cloying attempts to "achieve solidarity" within your own ranks that it's almost not worth doing. But then if you stay in one place long enough, you become part of the community—

like it or not—and eventually you have to pitch in, especially when the things that are going wrong where you are now are the same ones you had to escape from twenty-some years ago.

But politics is ugly, and it won't be long before you find yourself up a spiritual box canyon: You began with the best intentions, only to end up as ruthless as a paid assassin because that's what you have to do to win. So you have to wonder, Are those the only two choices: complete bastard or helpless victim? There are those who'll tell you not to let it get personal, but the dirtiest secret in politics is that it *is* personal.

And then there are those eerie reversals. One day someone asks you to annex into the town again, but this time it's not so they can gouge you for hook-up fees and taxes but so they can run you for mayor. You think, My God, are these people fools, or are things really that desperate?

Naturally, all of this can cut deeply into your fishing time.

Still, it *is* sometimes possible to achieve one single small thing that could make a difference, at least for the time being. When it comes right down to it, I hate politics as much as I love writing and fishing, but in all three of those endeavors it's possible to momentarily achieve the kind of clarity and precision you'll never see in your day-to-day life.

So I guess I've reached stage three in the long, slow process of becoming a bona fide local. Stage one was when no one knew or much cared who I was, and that went on for a long time, as it often does in small towns.

Stage two came when something clicked and people started speaking to me, usually asking how the fishing was.

Stage three came when I got involved in local politics

(always on the pro-environment, anti-growth side, of
course) and now, in some circles, I am known as "that son
of a bitch Gierach."

I don't mind that. I figure, if you think you're right and
you're making enemies of people you think are wrong,
you're doing okay. And anyway, it's sort of a family tradition. If you go to a certain small town in Wisconsin and ask
for that son of a bitch Gierach, you'll get directions to my
uncle Al's place.

I've written some stories about the little creek here (sometimes trying to disguise its name and location, though not
always successfully), and when I met a man who'd read
some of them, he said he was disappointed when he finally
saw and fished the thing. Interesting. I thought I'd described it pretty accurately, right down to the gas station
next door to the house, the cement plant on the stream and
the small trout you catch.

I like it, even though the trout aren't that big and parts
of it aren't entirely picturesque. That's because I've come
to believe that life isn't, can't be and probably shouldn't be
perfect, and that you'll be a lot happier if you live as much
the way you want to as possible, while at the same time
not having to cross every *t* and dot every *i*. But then I
suppose some romanticism inevitably creeps in when
you're talking about your favorite trout stream.

Then too, some of those stories go back a few years,
and although you don't always notice when you're right in
the middle of it, things do change.

The first Good Old Days parade I saw here consisted
of a flatbed truck full of drunks from the Sundance Saloon
with a hand-painted banner reading LIFE IN THE FAST LANE, a
handful of guys in buckskins from the local black-powder

gun club and the Pet Parade: a woman leading a golden retriever bitch that was clearly nursing, and four kids, each carrying a puppy.

They formed up in one block of Main Street and marched down the other block in front of an audience of twenty or thirty people. It was so much fun they went around the block and did it again. Then everyone went home except the drunks, who went back to the saloon.

Now, Good Old Days has a craft fair, flea market, carnival rides (cheap, little ones that don't look very safe), third-rate rock bands, loud cars, drunken fistfights and other elements of the full catastrophe. The city fathers and mothers are real proud of it, but a number of us make it a point to be out of town fishing the weekend it happens.

For a while the little sign you passed as you came into town said HOWDY, FOKS, but they changed it. I think someone realized it would only be funny if it was clear that the spelling error was intentional.

More to the point, down here on the lower stretch of the creek, there's more traffic than there used to be, more noise, more people fishing and so on. Don't get me wrong. It's still the Rocky Mountains and, compared to much of the country, it's pretty idyllic. But, still, it just ain't quite the same.

When I break down and complain about that (I try not to, but I'm only human), people sometimes ask me why I don't just move someplace where there are fewer people and better fishing. "In your line of work," a friend pointed out, "you could live anywhere. All you need is a phone and a mailbox and a generator for the word processor."

I do think about it sometimes. In the course of twenty years spent writing about fly-fishing, I've been to some neat places where—at first glance at least—it looks like a guy could live a quiet, pretty much undisturbed life with lots of space, few human neighbors, fish and game right out the back door and so on. It can be tempting, especially when you're experiencing that nervous, anything-could-happen freedom you feel when you're far from home.

Parts of western Montana are also not what they once were, but there are still some backwaters the movie stars haven't discovered yet. Wyoming, Utah, Idaho and, for that matter, parts of Colorado still have little one-horse, one-café, one-gas-station burgs that are near decent trout water but still nicely off the beaten path.

I really liked the Texas hill country north of San Antonio, with its rolling, forested hills, acres of wildflowers, polite people and lonesome limestone rivers full of bass and panfish, but then I was there in April, and I'm told the summers are kind of grim.

On the farther edge (unlikely, I suppose, but still sort of tantalizing) there's, let's say, King Salmon, Alaska, where there are fish the size of small canoes, or Goose Bay, Labrador, where one could spend time with some of the biggest brook trout in the world. Or, for less-terrifying winters, how about the bull trout and west-slope cutthroats around Fernie, British Columbia?

There's an interesting pattern here. All the places I'm thinking of have good fishing, but they don't have fly shops yet. I dearly love a good fly shop, but the presence of a new one is a symptom of growing popularity and all the nostalgic heartaches that come with it.

But then I keep coming back to the episode with the rock bass and all the other bits and pieces that would fit into the same category: things I know about now only because I've been kicking around here for twenty-five years, and I mean kicking around in a way I probably wouldn't do in a new place because I'd be in my late forties instead of my early twenties when I got there.

Not that I'm exactly a doddering old fool, but if you're in middle age yourself you know what I mean, and if you're in your twenties, trust me. If nothing else, you get a little smarter, take fewer risks, pace yourself better and run up fewer mountains just to see what the view is like.

Then again, you ran up some of those mountains once, so you already *know* what the view is like. Age doesn't necessarily bring wisdom, but you do build up a backlog of useful experience.

There are great fishing spots I know about and still go to, the likes of which I might not find in new country. And when I do go, I know—or at least have some ideas—about the best season, time of day, the weather, where to start, where to end up at dusk, approaches, tactics, fly patterns and I don't know what all else.

Sure, most of this is stuff that would work on any similar water, but I know from fishing similar water in other places that there's a subtle, intuitive, bioregional angle to it. A stream in British Columbia can be exactly like a stream here in northern Colorado in almost every way you can put your finger on, but I still fish the home water better. And it doesn't feel frozen in time the way a new stream can to a tourist who fishes it only once. If the home water is better or worse than it was ten years ago, I know that, and sometimes I can even tell you why.

Now, I'm not claiming to be such a great fisherman. In fact, that's probably the point. Without being a Dave Whitlock, Lefty Kreh, Joan Wulff or Dave Hughes, to name a few, and without knowing all that much about casting or entomology, I still do okay because I have a comfortable old familiarity with the place that fills in the large gaps in my skill with . . . Well, I don't know what exactly, but something just as useful.

I didn't even have to work at it in the way I usually understand that word. Sure, I've expended, and continue to expend, a lot of time and effort, and I do sometimes get deeply philosophical about it or claim I have to do it because it's my job, but I also love every minute of it.

My girlfriend Susan thinks it's interesting that, although most of my friends and I are fairly serious travelers, when we're *not* traveling we tend to be homebodies: apparently happy to kick around in a 20- or 30-mile radius of home, hang around the house and haunt the local cafés. There's always a little wanderlust in evidence, she says, but there's also a kind of satisfaction.

In the last year, two friends have told me they envied my sense of community. Both of these guys have spent the same years I've lived here moving restlessly from place to place, leaving behind pages in my address book with dozens of crossed out P.O. boxes and phone numbers. One of them, after a day's visit, said, "You know, I bet you've waved at or said hello to thirty people today."

A nice detail: one I wouldn't have noticed on my own. Luckily, on that particular day no one from the pro-growth side gave me the finger.

Now that I think about it, I also know who's a good carpenter, fly tier, rod maker, auto mechanic and gunsmith; who'll return a favor and who won't; which café makes the best coffee and where I might even be able to get a free cup now and then: the same sorts of things I know about the fishing.

So maybe I don't move because I'm lazy. Or maybe by now I enjoy the familiarity of it all as much as anything else, and I'm afraid it would take me the rest of my life to get back to the same thing somewhere else—or that I'd never get it back at all.

And anyway, if I did move it would probably take my new neighbors a decade or more to recognize me, take me in and then finally realize I'm an outside agitator and a son of a bitch.

3

Folk Art

Ed Engle, Steve Peterson, Larry Pogreba and I had bought a day on a pay-to-fish private spring creek in Montana, one of the famous ones in the Paradise Valley, near

Livingston. This is the kind of treat we'll sometimes decide to give ourselves for no other reason than that we're going to be in that part of Montana anyway and can all afford the rod fees at the same time.

I can't speak for Steve and Larry because they'd been off on their own somewhere, but Ed and I were only a few days into the trip and were just beginning to run up against a little sleep deprivation. Nothing serious yet—no need to declare a camp day to sleep in, have a big breakfast, wash out some socks and then doze under a tree with a book until noon. Still, a little minor road burn always creeps in, even on those trips where you promise each other you'll take it easy this time.

We'd all met at a campground on the Yellowstone River the night before. I don't remember where Steve and Larry were coming from, but they pulled in well after dark and woke us up.

Before that, just about the time Ed and I were turning in, a few pickup loads of cowboys had pulled in nearby and launched into what we used to call a "woodsy." That's a spur-of-the-moment party where a bunch of people drive out into the country to build a huge fire, drink beer, yell, discharge firearms into the air and so on. In some parts of the world this is considered a valid and harmless form of therapy, and, having been a participant in a few, I can vouch for that. A woodsy can be aggravating as hell if you're not actually taking part in it—and sometimes you can't help but wonder where some of those stray rounds are landing—but if you were young once, you let it go, stuff in some ear plugs and try to sleep through it.

I did drift off finally—the way you can if you're tired enough, even though someone in the next room is watching a loud war movie on TV—but I couldn't have been out for more than an hour when Steve and Larry pulled in, flashing a spotlight through the pale blue wall of my tent and bolting me awake, thinking I was about to either relive a scene from *Deliverance* or get busted by the local sheriff for God knows what.

So then, of course, we had to help set up Larry's elaborate, homemade fold-out camper, hear about their trip so far, tell about some highlights from ours and so on, all just happy to see each other. After all, when two parties of fishermen on separate driving trips plan to meet at a certain campground on a certain evening, it can begin to seem like a pretty unlikely rendezvous. Two courses, each several days and hundreds of miles long, have to converge at a single spot at a single time, cheating the combined forces of breakdowns, accidents, emergency detours and just plain getting lost on strange roads in the dark.

When someone *doesn't* show up—and that's been known to happen—you have to think, This could be serious. It's fishing, after all, and you don't just change your mind. When Larry is one of the people involved, you can always say, "Well, he probably got distracted by a junkyard or a farm auction," but then in the back of your mind you also have to think, Jeez, I hope they're not dead.

So when they finally did come dragging in at something like three in the morning, there were a few camp chores and a little celebration. By breakfast, we'd all had maybe two or three fitful hours of sleep, tops, and we hit the spring creek wired on coffee and a little edgy, which is actually not a bad state to be in for some meticulous dry fly fishing.

This was somewhere around the first week of June. The Pale Morning Dun mayflies were starting to come off pretty well, but the hatch wasn't in full swing yet, so there weren't as many fisherpersons on the water as there could have been, just one couple besides the four of us.

The morning was ideal for dry fly fishing—chilly, still and overcast, with a light drizzle coming and going—but by early afternoon the cold front had piled up and stalled against the Gallatin Range. It had turned colder and started to rain seriously, so we'd retired to the fishermen's hut for a lunch and weather break.

You pay to fish a spring creek for the big trout and great hatches, not for amenities, but this fisherman's hut is a nice, European touch. It's not fancy, but it's dry and, once you get a fire together, it's warm, too.

We had a good blaze going in the cast-iron stove and a pot of coffee on when half of the couple we were sharing the creek with—the woman—walked in. The hatch had gone off, but presumably the man was still out there grimly nymphing in the rain.

Ed and I were wolfing sandwiches, talking loudly with our mouths full and otherwise not exhibiting the best table manners, while Steve and Larry were standing by the stove, waders down around their ankles, toasting their backsides. Steve's long johns were faded red, Larry's had once been white and both had some pretty substantial holes in them. (After all, you don't wear the dress long johns on a fishing trip.) There was nothing actually obscene about it, but, you know, there were nonetheless gaping holes in the underwear, revealing hairy male anatomy.

We were engaged in a spirited discussion about carp. The day before, Steve and Larry had spent the afternoon hooking big carp on flies off a high bridge somewhere. It was the only way they could get a good drift over the fish, they said, but there was no way they could land them, so they just played them for a while and then broke them off.

Ed wanted to know why they didn't climb down from

the bridge and play the fish from the bank. Steve said
they'd thought of that, but the bridge was too high and the
bank was too steep.

"I guess I wasn't into risking my life to land a carp,"
Larry added.

"Why not?" Ed asked.

I wanted to know what flies they were using, what
kind of drift and how the fish were taking. Violently? Lazily?
Fly-fishing for carp is an obscure business, so any new
information is welcome.

"They were really cool carp," Steve said. "I bet some
of 'em went 20, 25 pounds."

"Yeah, easy," Larry said. Then he turned to the
woman, who'd been standing there in the open doorway,
rainwater dripping from her hat, and said, "Hi."

"Hi," she answered with the uncertainty of someone
who has accidentally wandered into the wrong neighborhood. Then she found a chair in the corner, picked up an
old fishing magazine and began paging through it.

"You wanna turnip?" Steve asked her, holding out a
big, sickly white tuber.

Steve doesn't eat turnips as a joke or to make a point
about macrobiotics, he actually likes them, and on this trip
he had a whole large cooler full of them, which he had
lugged into the hut.

"These are good, strong ones," he told the woman.
"They make your lips tingle."

"No thank you," she said, a little coldly, I thought.

We asked her how she'd done that morning, what flies
they'd been using, where they were from and such, but
after a few terse, one-word answers we realized she was
trying to ignore us and decided the most polite thing to do
was return the favor.

That was okay with me. I've always thought courtesy

was overrated, and that if you don't feel like talking to people you don't like, you shouldn't have to.

Maybe she was tired or bored or just uncomfortable crammed into a small hut with four strange men. Or maybe she thought that when you paid a $50-a-day rod fee on a fancy spring creek you could expect to meet a better class of people and be offered elk pâté instead of raw turnips; hear more talk about dry flies and brown trout and less about carp. I guess it's even possible that Larry had made a bad first impression when they'd met earlier in the day.

It had been a fine morning, as I said. The hatch wasn't especially heavy, but it was long and steady; there were enough flies on the water to get the trout good and interested, and the cool, damp weather kept the duns on the surface for a long time before their wings dried and they could fly off.

The fish were your typical catch-and-release spring creek trout: browns and rainbows as plump and healthy as hothouse tomatoes and no pushovers. They were rising to the little duns with the casual, unhurried confidence of fish who have it good, know it and think they deserve it. Sometimes they'd spook at a bad cast, but they were just as likely to calmly sink down a foot or two in the clear water and sulk, clearly more annoyed than frightened.

They'd refuse a poorly drifted fly and, even though it was still early in the season, many of them seemed suspicious of the little post-wing thorax duns that are the standard pattern for this hatch. By standard I mean it's the fly you automatically start with, although the one you eventually catch fish on (assuming you do catch some) can be something else entirely.

This whole business of the perfect fly presented flawlessly to rising trout is why you go to some trouble and expense to fish a great spring creek. You're trying to have the courage of your convictions. As a fly fisher you're supposed to love a challenge—love it so much that you'll pay for it, even with hundreds of miles of free public water in the neighborhood. If you're a competent fisherman having a decent day, you can usually manage a few big trout. On a bad day you can at least know that getting skunked on a spring creek puts you in the same class with some of the world's best fly casters (whether they'll admit that or not).

Ed, Steve and I were doing okay, catching some fish on light rods and small dry flies, as one is expected to do on water like this, and Larry was doing what he likes to do, which is to go about it all wrong but catch fish anyway.

Well, maybe "all wrong" isn't exactly what I mean. In fact, Larry is what you'd have to call a great fly fisherman of the old Rocky Mountain school. He's up on all the current, technical stuff, but at heart he's a practical, instinctive angler who through much of his life has fly fished as much for food as for sport. I've noticed that guys like that have a kind of goofy, predatory edge we pure-sport types usually lack.

And he's also one of those born experimenters: He taught himself about blacksmithing and metallurgy and now hand-forges Damascus-steel knives, he makes guitars, builds cabins, raises game birds, repairs and sometimes redesigns automobiles and so on. He does so many things well that those of us who know him are seldom surprised anymore, although we're still sometimes amazed.

For instance, Larry once built a car from the ground up: the only Pogrebamobile in existence. At first glance it

looks like a cross between a silver dune buggy and a for-
mula racer. It has a chrome trout hood ornament and goes
very fast, although Larry is always trying to make it go a
little faster yet.

He believes that a broken item that's imaginatively
patched has a lot more style than a new one and also,
apparently, that things can always be done another way.

If guys like this could afford to fool around with space
travel, we'd have cities on Mars and warp drive by now.

More to the point, when Larry finds that trout can be
caught on, say, a size 18 Pale Morning Dun thorax dry fly,
he immediately wonders what *else* they might be caught
on. A Royal Wulff? A streamer? A bigger streamer? What
about a fluorescent pink rubber squid left over from a trip
to Belize?

He seems especially eager to try things like this on
catch-and-release water. I mean, if you have to put the fish
back anyway, why not try something strange just to see
what happens, in the spirit of vernacular pure science?

By now this approach to things has evolved into something like an art form. Larry has some interesting ideas
about art as life and vice versa, but I won't try to go into
them in any detail here. Suffice it to say that he's been
known to accumulate ridiculous fly patterns not only because he knows he can catch fish on them, but because he
likes the statement that will make.

Before I met Larry I'd never fished with anyone who
had this degree of playful curiosity. Almost every other fly
fisher I've known (and me too, for that matter) just wanted
to figure out what the fish were taking, arrive at something
like the correct pattern and then catch as many as possible.
If you tied the fly yourself, so much the better, but even
picking the right one out of a bin down at the fly shop is

something you can take credit for. You can say, "It just kinda jumped out at me."

Either way, the more fish you catch, the more convincing the proof that the fly and the tactic you settled on were the right and proper ones.

I've come to think of this as the place-tab-A-into-slot-B school of fly-fishing, and there's nothing wrong with it, but Larry seems more interested in locating the edges of the envelope than in just catching a lot of fish in the accepted manner. It's fascinating to watch—and you'd be amazed at how often the rubber squid works.

So that morning, using a rod many would say is way too heavy for a little spring creek, Larry was fishing a large, bright yellow Pistol Pete through a perfect, delicate mayfly hatch and catching more and bigger fish than anyone else.

A Pistol Pete, by the way, is a Woolly Worm with a brass propeller on its nose, a kind of rig that's out of style now, but that you'll find mentioned in old fishing books in which the authors talked about catching your limit and included recipes. I've never seen one in a fly shop, but you can find them in many hardware stores, usually right next to the worm cooler.

I appreciate people who fish like that, because they help keep me honest. I know myself too well, and I have to admit that if I'd fallen in with the wrong company at the wrong time, I'd probably have become a snob myself. As it is, I have this thing for fine tackle and this tendency to think flies that float are somehow morally superior to ones that sink. But having a friend like Larry—with his torn bluejeans; battered, oil-stained baseball cap and "Dracula Sucks" T-shirt—reminds me that all snobbery is defensive and that, as important as fishing seems, the most important thing about it is, it's just fishing.

Of course there are some anglers who don't see it that way.

Around midmorning I was casting to a pod of four or five good-sized trout when I spotted Larry working his way downstream. (Larry seldom pounds a single lie for long. He prefers to cover water, looking for the fish that will bite rather than fooling around with the ones that won't.) In a hundred yards or so I saw him land four trout, each 20 inches or better.

Then he ran into the couple. They were fishing close together, apparently consulting often and in great detail about insects and fly patterns. Larry had gotten out of the water and was walking around them on shore so as to give them plenty of room, but the man waved and they stopped to talk. I was too far away to hear the conversation, but I could tell how it went by the body language.

The man asked, "What are you using?" expecting to hear about something like a cul de canard, half-spent, crippled Pale Morning Dun emerger with one wing folded into the trailing nymphal husk.

Larry held up his fly and said, "Size 8 Pistol Pete."

The man's face went blank—I mean, a thing like that isn't supposed to work on a spring creek, is it? And even if it does, isn't it, well, unacceptable?

Larry, sensing weakness, explained that you could get Pistol Petes at the feed store in town, that they only cost 75 cents and that they held up a lot better than them little mayfly patterns.

That's only a guess because, as I said, I was too far away to hear, but I do know Larry and I'd seen him do this kind of thing before.

The couple seemed dumbfounded—possibly even a

little scandalized—and I've seen *that* before, too. Maybe I'm just getting old, but it seems like a lot of fly fishers these days have lost the capacity for delight and the ability to kid around.

One thing I *could* tell—even at that range—was that the woman was staring hard at Larry's T-shirt, which features Dracula biting the neck of a near-naked woman whose bare ass is padded to produce a startling 3-D effect. It's in pretty bad taste, I guess, unless after careful consideration you've determined that a certain kind of bad taste qualifies as folk art.

CHAPTER

4

Solitude

*I*t's surprising how seldom I fish alone, considering how much I enjoy it. Well, okay, in the sense that fly-fishing isn't a team sport and it's not competitive, you *always* fish alone, even when you're casting from the same boat with another fisherman and a guide, but you know what I mean. I mean by myself, without arrangements or conversation, without even seeing another human, if I'm lucky.

That's not to say I don't like fishing with other people. Nine times out of ten it's the folks more than the fish that define the character of a trip, and among my fly-fishing friends there are some who define character in distinctive ways.

As unfair as it is to sum people up in a phrase or two, I'll say that Steve fishes hard without being obnoxious about it and continues to wear neon colors no matter what anyone says; Ed approaches fish and water with a weird kind of detached curiosity and seems to be on a perpetual guide's day off; Mike Price delights in going to notoriously difficult rivers during highly technical hatches and catching fish on a Royal Coachman; Mike Clark is usually just happy to be casting—instead of painstakingly *making*—bamboo fly rods; A.K. is a good-natured purist who thinks everything that happens on a fishing trip amounts to poetic justice and so on.

If pressed, I think all those guys would agree that fly-fishing eventually causes you to look into your own soul, but I'm probably the only one among us who would actually say something like that with a straight face. When I try too hard to be profound, none of these guys are shy about telling me to cram it, but I don't think any of them realize what a great service that is.

A trip with any one of these people has a distinct flavor —without being predictable—and a trip with any combination of them can turn out like a good Brunswick stew made from high-quality leftovers.

And then there are the strangers: people you bump into on the water in those offhand encounters that can make your day, piss you off or mean nothing at all. There was a man I used to run into on the South Platte River all the time. I never knew his name, but I always thought of him as The Gentleman. We never spoke, we'd just nod or wave and otherwise give each other plenty of room, neither of us wanting to intrude on the other's solitude or have ours intruded upon. I saw him maybe a dozen times a season for about two years and I haven't seen him since. He was a young guy, so maybe he just moved away.

And there's that first-date sensation you get meeting a guide you've never fished with before; you size each other up, each wondering if the other has a clue, both knowing you'll find out soon enough. And there's the sense of re-union when you hook up with a guide you *have* fished with before and you're doing it again because he was so good the last time. You remember what a fine job he did. He remembers that you tipped okay and didn't fall out of the boat.

Friends of friends can be interesting, too. Sometimes they're great, but just as often they're lushes, whiners, fish hogs or fascists and you end up asking the friend who brought them, "Now, this guy is actually an old *pal* of yours, is that right?"

Sometimes people you think you know can also turn out to be strangers of a sort. Have you ever gone fishing for the first time with someone you've known forever in more polite circumstances and found yourself adjusting your opinion of them one way or the other? Have you ever had someone pitch a deal on a bass pond or try to sell you real estate during a Red Quill hatch?

I sometimes even fish with an old-guard Reagan Re-publican—on his private water, of course. It's always fun, although I think there are times when we both view these trips as acts of charity.

But when it comes right down to it, I guess I have to admit I'm not all that fond of people in general—if nothing else, there are too damned many of them—although the occasional good ones are so delightful they do sometimes seem to make up for all the schmucks.

Still, there are times when I want to get away from the whole species for a while. A New Age type I know once pointedly told me that what we don't like about other people are usually the same things we don't like about ourselves. Okay, fine, but a guy can still take a break, can't he?

I do most of my solitary fishing near home. Sometimes I'll drive out to a bluegill pond or a local lake for a few hours: someplace where I may well run into someone I know, and that's usually okay. It's usually even okay if we end up fishing together for the afternoon and then meet at some joint for supper. In the long run, fishermen are better company than most. If nothing else, most of them don't feel obliged to fill up normal moments of silence with meaningless chatter.

But if I really want to be alone, I'll take a day and do one of the small mountain trout streams up in the national forest or wilderness area: streams that require a fair amount of four-wheeling, and then some walking, to reach stretches where the fish aren't that big anyway and where, consequently, it really is rare to run into anyone.

Naturally, I take the normal precaution of having someone know roughly where I went, or at least of tacking a note on my front door, so that in the unlikely event I break a leg and need to be rescued it won't take someone two weeks to figure that out.

I try to be mindful of my motivation when I go off alone. I mean, if you're weary, sick but still ambulatory, fed up, overworked, angry, frustrated, heartbroken, need to think things over or need to *stop* thinking things over for a while, you should definitely go fishing, and you should probably go alone so you don't bother anyone. But then fishing, like most other simple human pleasures, is better when it's done out of love than when it's used as a painkiller.

Of course things aren't always simple. I've gone fishing alone a few times because it was either that or resort to violence, and as it turned out, fishing was usually the better choice. It's not that I'm exactly opposed to the idea of revenge, but, as the old Italian saying goes, it's a dish best served cold. If I'm still pissed after a day of fishing, I know I should start planning to do something about it.

It's not likely for a solitary trip to end in a great epiphany or anything, it's just that I think the way you fish when you're alone is the way you really fish: your own personal style, uninfluenced by crowds, guides or friends, and it's interesting to plug back into that now and then. Solitude is educational and it *can* be satisfying. For instance, I've lived alone off and on for better than half my adult life and have found myself to be decent company.

Apparently, my true calling is to fish dry flies with a bamboo rod, even to the point of leaving the nymph box at home, because that's what I do when I'm by myself. Of course the trout in these little pocket-water, freestone streams do rise freely whether there's a hatch on or not, but carrying nothing but dry flies still makes me feel pretty stylish.

The rod I've been using lately doesn't hurt, either. It's a little $7\frac{1}{2}$-foot, 5-weight F. E. Thomas Special bamboo, circa 1940, that casts a short line beautifully. Normally a rod like this could be considered too good to bang around on a rough stream, but this one has been refinished and one tip is down an inch, which moves it neatly from the museum piece into the nice old fishin' pole category.

I wear hip waders because it's rare to wade more than knee-deep in these little creeks, but I usually do a lot of walking, and the old boot-foot jobs I used to use have been known to get uncomfortable and even raise blisters. So now I have a pair of those neoprene hippers that take a lace-up wading shoe. They're a little more of a production to get into and out of, but they fit better, and footwear is the hiker's most valuable tool.

Otherwise I travel as lightly as possible, but I still carry a sheath knife, waterproof matchbox, water purification tablets and an empty canteen (to keep the weight down), coffeepot, tin cup and a few other odds and ends, including a simple lunch.

Once in a great while I bring the sandwich home at the end of the day, having dined instead on raspberries, wild mushrooms and a brace of small brook trout roasted on a stick. That's one of the great meals of all time, but it does take some effort to put together.

Even if I just wolf down the sandwich and a piece of fruit, I almost always find a pretty spot and take an elaborate coffee break, if only because I carried the coffeepot a couple of miles and am, by God, gonna use it. I own a small, lightweight backpack stove, but on trips like this I prefer an open spruce fire with the coffeepot suspended over it on a stick. I've long since graduated from the old wood, canvas and steel school of woodcraft I knew as a kid, where you cleared brush, dug drainage ditches, felled trees for a lean-to and otherwise conquered the wilderness, but I do still like a little fire.

After coffee, I put the pot in a plastic bag before stashing it in the day pack. That keeps the soot from the fire off of all the other stuff. Not that it would matter much, but in the woods, unlike at home, I like to be neat and efficient.

I think I walk more, cast less, spend more time distracted and take longer breaks when I'm alone, but I can't be absolutely sure of that. Trying to remember it now, from a desk chair, it seems like I'm less aware of my own pace when I'm alone, so maybe that's the difference. When I've been out with partners or guides, I can tell you in no uncertain terms if it was lazy or frantic or somewhere in between.

I think I also see more when I'm alone, although, again, I don't know if that's an accurate recollection or not. It seems like there's more scenery, weather, wildlife and birdsong in my head at the end of a solitary day, but maybe that's just because that space isn't filled up with conversation and other people's fish. My memory isn't exactly poor, but it does seem to have a limited capacity.

But I suppose it's really the fishing that sets the pace, as always. If the trout aren't rising, I'll cruise, working the good-looking water with a Royal Wulff or a hopper, or maybe something slightly more exotic, like a Roy Palm–style crane fly.

The trout in these little streams are usually curious, aggressive and just plain hungry, so any number of dry flies will work, but I'll still fool around with patterns until I find the one that, on that particular day, really rattles their cages. It's funny what that turns out to be sometimes.

If the trout *are* rising, my natural tendency is to try to match what the trout are eating, because that's how we do it now, but up there it's likely to be one of those sparse, mixed, multiple hatch/spinner fall deals where a #14 Wulff will work as well as anything else and be a lot easier to see.

Ed says that's what he likes about freestone streams, as opposed to the classier tailwaters and spring creeks. They're pretty much nontechnical, and all that stuff from the old fly-fishing books still works.

•

One of the best things about being alone is that if you put down a big fish (a big fish here would be a foot long or more—but not much more) you can stop and rest the water if you feel like it, or even leave it and come back in an hour.

I can remember when it was a standard item of courtesy among fly fishers to let someone rest a pool. ("Resting the water is the same as fishing it," my friend Koke Winter once said in that way he has that leaves no room for discussion. "In fact, it's the mark of a competent angler.") But now, at least on a lot of crowded rivers, there'll be another guy in your spot before you even find a comfortable rock to sit on, so your only two choices are to keep casting where you are or move on.

Well, there's a third choice, which is to try to give the guy a lesson in streamside etiquette, but that's a touchy business. My problem is, if I'm worked up enough to actually get into it, I'll begin with something like, "Listen here, you ignorant shit. . . ," which is usually not productive.

I suppose people rush spots like that out of a sense of self-defense, because there are those who'll grab a good hole and camp on it all day, or even try to crowd you out when you start catching fish. I've been on rivers where a real gentleman would end up standing on the bank all day.

At its best, courtesy is like a chess game. At worst, it's like too many hungry rats in a small cage. Having a whole stream to yourself for a day means that, for once, you don't even have to think about it. Plus, you can talk to yourself, pee where you like, scratch where it itches, laugh at particularly amusing rocks, yell at birds and otherwise relax in a profound way.

I don't know if I really see more clearly, cast better, miss fewer strikes and play fish with greater finesse when

I'm alone or not. I guess it doesn't matter, because that's how I remember it, and there are no witnesses.

The last time I was out alone I had a great day. The stretch of creek I was fishing had a nice mix of browns and brookies, and there were all kinds of bugs around, from #10 or #12 Green Drakes and Yellow Caddis down to some little Blue Dun mayflies. I'd spent half the morning switching patterns and finally settled on a #14 Flavilinea mayfly with dun hackle and white goat-hair wings.

I caught lots of trout, most small, but a few up around 12 inches and one chubby brown that might have gone 14. I was having so much fun that by four o'clock I hadn't stopped for coffee yet.

I was just thinking about that—looking for a comfortable spot for a twig fire—when I came on a long stretch of jumbled pocket water that ran out of the sunlight into a tunnel of overhanging spruce and willow. It was dark and steep in there, with what looked like some deep pools, and silhouetted against the sunlit trees at the far end I could see caddis and mayflies in the air. Okay, I thought, coffee later.

I got up on the slope a little, into the more open forest, and hiked down to the bottom end of this stretch so I could fish it upstream. The bank was an unwalkable tangle of trunks and brush, so I got into the water, and I'd been right, the pools *were* deep. This was actually a step beyond pocket water, but not quite a cascade. It was more of a chute, where the water tumbled over and around boulders into small, stair-stepping, braided pools.

Dry fly drifts and back casts were both tricky in there, but if I could drop a fly into the bubbly white water at the head of a plunge, a trout would hammer it as soon as it drifted into a clear current.

Moving from one pool to the next was a matter of scrambling over boulders and deadfalls while wearing hip boots and a pack, which I've never seen anyone do gracefully. I probably wasn't as careful with the old cane rod as some collector friends would have liked, but I think I was as careful as the late Mr. Thomas would have expected, seeing as how there were fish to be caught.

And then a neat thing happened. I flipped a cast to the head of a plunge pool and watched it bob down in the current. It was such a pretty drift that when the fly went completely out of sight behind a big rock, I just let it go, and while it was back there I got this feeling that I should set the hook, so I did. And of course there was a fish on.

I don't know if it was luck or clairvoyance, but it was pretty cool, even though it only turned out to be a 7-inch brookie.

Oddly enough, my first reaction was to look around to see if anyone was watching. I knew I was alone—I'd gone to great pains to be—but I guess I wished someone had been there to see it.

CHAPTER

5

Splake

*L*ast year Mike Clark and I went fishing for splake in a little mountain lake in Colorado's Arapaho National Forest. It was a simple case of fly fisher's curiosity: We learned that these fish had been quietly planted there a few years before by the Division of Wildlife (without fanfare or a press release), and since neither of us had ever caught one and the lake was only a few hours' drive from home, we figured we'd better check it out.

A splake is a hybrid fish made by crossing a brook trout with a lake trout: the kind of thing people do because they can, and because they just can't leave well enough alone. These fish were first produced in the 1870s by the legendary New York fish culturist Seth Green, but they didn't start to become popular until the 1940s, when they were experimentally planted in British Columbia. In Canada, a brookie is sometimes called a speckled trout. The name "splake" comes from the *sp* in "speckled" tacked onto the *lake* in "lake trout." It's not a very pretty name, but I guess it could have been worse.

The brook trout × lake trout hybrid is not one that occurs in nature like, say, the cutthroat × rainbow, known as a cuttbow, but once produced artificially the splake is an unusual hybrid because it can and does spawn successfully. Splake—horny little devils, apparently—will mate with each other and they'll also backcross, breeding with either lake trout or brook trout.

Ask a fisheries biologist about this and he may wander off into the relative viability of the eggs from a splake × splake cross versus those of the original lake trout × brook trout mating or the varied appearance of the young resulting from the (splake × brook trout) × brook trout cross and so on.

You'll listen patiently because, after all, you *did* ask, but the upshot is, after a few generations in wild water with pure-strain fish, the splakes' genetics can get a little muddy. I want to picture that as the wild genes trying to reassert themselves, but there may be more poetry than science to that.

As some fisheries managers see it, a splake has at least two advantages as a sport fish: It has a faster initial growth rate than a lake trout—which means it gets to catchable size quicker—and in most waters it tends to be larger at maturity than a brook trout.

According to Jim Satterfield, the biologist responsible for stocking splake where Mike and I fished for them, these critters can also be used to control runaway populations of stunted brook trout. Splake will feed on insects, crustaceans and such, but they also share the lake trouts' aggressiveness and taste for small fish.

"Putting splake into a brook trout lake is a lot like putting bass into a bluegill pond," Satterfield said. "The idea is to achieve the proper predator/prey balance."

Sure, perfect balances can't always be achieved by stocking (and they don't always happen in nature, either), but Satterfield said that under ideal conditions some of the once small, stunted brook trout in a little high-altitude lake with a short growing season could get to be 16 inches long, and the larger splake might weigh in at 3 or 4 pounds. All of which sounds pretty good, at least on paper.

The thing is, I've always had some nagging misgivings about designer fish. It's nothing I can lay out in a coherent argument, it just seems like there are enough *real* fish around that you shouldn't have to cross white bass with striped bass to get wipers or fertilize the eggs of northern pike with the milt of muskellunge (or is it the other way around?) to get tiger muskies. If that kind of thing was supposed to happen, it would have happened on its own. Since it didn't, maybe there's a reason.

Some fisheries managers like these artificial hybrids because most of the fish are sterile, so populations can be controlled with great precision and, with only one age class in the water at a time, they can be grown to large size quickly, like cattle in a feedlot. If they're stocked properly, the biologists say, they won't push any other fish out of their deserved niches, and, as a friend of mine once pointed out, "Some of these impoundment fisheries are so artificial they might as *well* be full of cowalskis." (Just in case you haven't heard that old joke, a cowalski is a coho/walleye/muskie hybrid that doesn't know how to swim.)

Still, I can't completely shake the suspicion that the engineering of unnatural creatures is a selfishly vain business—not unlike having high-priced fertility clinics in a society that's already overpopulated—and maybe even a little dangerous in a 1950s horror movie sort of way. If you watched those things religiously, as I did as a kid, you'll know that monstrosities sooner or later turn on their creators in awful and unpredictable ways. I can't say what might happen with these peculiar fish, but I can picture that obligatory scene in *The Wiper That Ate Denver,* where the earnest young fly fisherman says to the wild-eyed fisheries biologist, "You crossed a *what* with a *what?* My God man, are you *mad?!*"

On the other hand, I've been trying to fight my natural tendency to be a tight-lipped prude about anything new and, for the record, I'm not one of those who wants to see nothing but indigenous fish in their native waters. After all, here in Colorado we have maybe twenty-some species of game fish (the actual number depends on how eclectic your tastes are), and all but the cutthroat trout and whitefish were introduced. I love it here and I sometimes pine for the old days, but I wonder how happy I'd have been catching whitefish, squawfish, chubs, suckers and the occasional cutt.

I've never quite gotten around to trying for the local tiger muskies, even though I'm told they get huge and can be caught on standard pike flies. A guy I know who *has* caught them says they grow bigger than northerns, but lack the famous reticence of muskies, so you can actually hook one now and then.

I did once go after wipers in what I thought was a nice, open-minded sort of way. I couldn't find any and, instead, ended up catching some good-sized rainbow trout on damselflies, which was kind of a relief.

Those trout had been in the water for a few years, but, like the wipers, they were also hatchery fish with questionable pedigrees living in a lake that had once been a low spot in a pasture. Still, under the right conditions the rainbows could spawn. Now that I think about it, maybe that's all it is. Maybe I just can't relate to a fish that doesn't have a sex life.

So anyway, Mike and I strapped my canoe on top of the pickup and ground our way up to the splake lake on a series of steep, rocky four-wheel-drive roads. It was a chilly day with a dense fog settled in at about 7,000 feet, so when we found the lake it gave the impression of stretching to the horizon, even though it was set in a small cirque and only covered about 30 or 40 acres.

There was some evidence of people having been there —old fire pits, a few faded beer cans—but it was mid-week, and there was no one else on the road and no one at the lake.

We launched the canoe after hanging a bright orange rain slicker on the canoe rack so we could find the truck again in the fog. What we could see of the lake's surface was dull, glassy and vacant looking—like a mirror reflecting another mirror—and there were some scattered rises here and there, the kind of lazy swirls fish make when they're eating bugs that are just sitting there being easy targets.

All we could see on the water were a few size 18 or so midges, so we started with #18 Royal Wulffs with the same size Hare's Ear soft hackles on short droppers; the kind of standard, businesslike high-lake rig you'd use for, say, brook trout or cutthroats—not exact, but usually close enough.

Mike caught the first fish—maybe a 7 or 8 incher—and we both had a look at it.

Satterfield had coached us a little on identification. He said that at first glance a splake looks an awful lot like a brookie—and there would still probably be some brookies in there—but on closer examination you'll notice that the wormlike markings on the back of the splake are larger, the snout is more elongated, the white fin margins aren't as prominent and, although a splake may have an orange cast to the belly like a brook trout, the red spots on the body are missing. The initial effect is subliminal. You think, This is a sickly-looking brook trout, without quite being able to put your finger on why.

But the real diagnostic mark is the tail. The tail of a brook trout is nearly flat (they call them squaretails in the East), while the tail of a splake is noticeably forked. This lake carries a limit of two splake 14 inches or better and, fine anatomical points aside, that's how the Wildlife officers tell the difference. So if it has a forked tail, the fish had better be 14 inches long, and you'd better not have more than two of them.

There had once been a sign posted at the lake with the regulations on it, along with a little essay on splake and brook trout, but some fun-loving locals had chained it up to a jeep and dragged it off. I guess I don't understand that. It seems to me a poacher with real guts would break the rules while leaving them posted. Stealing the sign so you can claim ignorance if you get caught is more of a lawyer's trick.

We looked the fish over quickly—in less time than it just took to tell about it, I think—and then let it go. It had clearly been a small splake, and I asked Mike, "Well, what do you think of them?"

"I don't know," he said, "I guess they're pretty cool. What d'*you* think?"

"Well," I said, "it was definitely a fish."

All in all, it was a normal kind of mountain-lake day. We drifted around in the canoe, casting to occasionally rising fish, catching a few and just enjoying the scene.

I'm almost always pleased just to be in a canoe—especially *my* canoe, which I'm very fond of—and the lake was especially gorgeous that day. If we were close to shore, jumbled granite boulders or dark stands of spruce would loom and dissolve as the thick fog shifted, and I felt like part of a Sung Dynasty Chinese watercolor. Out in more open water the fog was just a disorienting gray dome with no horizon, where the rings of rises seemed to float in the air and ranges were deceptive. The rises were closer than they appeared, and it was easy to cast too far.

Between us, we caught maybe twenty splake up to about a foot long, on small flies and light bamboo rods. They stayed near the surface to fight, unlike lake trout, which want to dive for the bottom when they feel the hook. Then we tried some streamers and weighted nymphs, hoping for bigger fish, but didn't get so much as a bump. Satterfield had told us that a recent netting survey showed there were some keepers in there, as well as a handful of splake up around 17 or 18 inches.

Somewhere in there I landed a real brook trout. It was the smallest fish of the day, but beautiful, and I said to Mike, "Look at this."

"All right," he said, "that's nice."

Just a few days before, we'd gone to another lake nearby where we'd caught and released a mess of 16-inch lake trout taken on dry flies. (Before lakers turn to a fish diet, belly out and sink toward the bottom, they act just like cutthroats.) So in less than a week we had, in effect, caught pure lake trout, pure brookies and their improbable offspring. I couldn't help feeling that the real fish were more, I don't know . . . authentic, I guess—the products of millions of years of evolution instead of one afternoon at the hatchery.

That's not to say the splake weren't fun. I mean, they were troutlike fish eating flies in a pretty mountain lake: the kind of thing that's perfectly okay unless you think too much. I *do* think too much at times, but I tend to do it at home. On the water, I'm usually able to just fish and be happy.

That's part of a conscious effort I've been making. I think you have to have your ideals and even speak up for them, but it's probably a good idea to pick your fights so you're not fighting *all* the time, and otherwise try to get along in the world as it is. (And if you also want to bury some ammunition and canned goods in the backyard just in case, okay.)

If pressed, I can picture a world where the wild critters are all gone, and if we fish at all we'll be after big, dumb, test-tube creations that look and act a lot like domestic turkeys. It might be okay if you don't remember what it used to be like, but the loss will be very real.

You have to do what you can to keep that and other horrors from happening, but at the same time too much lusting after perfection will make you nuts, in which case your own life is ruined and you're no help to your cause. You must avoid becoming that guy you read about in the papers now and then. When he was finally carted off to an institution, the Health Department found that he'd been living with sixty cats and several raccoons without the benefit of litter boxes and had saved all his newspapers since 1953. His baseball cap was lined with tin foil to ward off alien radio signals, and he was mumbling something about mutant fish trying to control his mind.

We never did crack that 14-inch limit on the splake—even after going back and trying again a week later—and I really want to do that because I'd like to eat one, which I would do without a second thought. If I continue fishing for splake, I'll probably release them as matter-of-factly as I do almost everything else, but for some reason I first want to see if they taste the way they fight, that is, more like a brookie than a lake trout.

That's one advantage, I guess. In a world where killing and eating a wild trout can pose a gut-wrenching dilemma, a designer fish has about the same moral weight as a hotdog.

6

Lost Rod

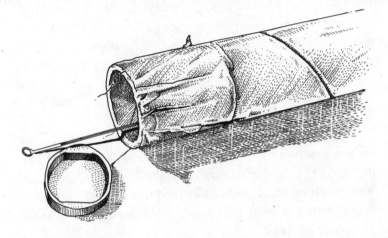

Not long ago I lost a bamboo fly rod, or, to call a spade a spade, I had a rod stolen. The maker, George Maurer of Kutztown, Pennsylvania, shipped it to me on a Monday. The following Monday (a day or two longer than it should have taken) the empty shipping tube arrived on my front porch in Colorado. It took a few seconds to sink in, but, sure enough, one end of the tube had been opened neatly with a sharp knife and there was nothing inside. It wasn't a mistake and it wasn't a joke. Maurer's sense of humor is a little odd, but he wouldn't do something like that.

I called him just to make sure. He thought *I* was kidding.

Naturally, it was a great rod: an 8-foot, 5-weight bamboo with a lovely, powerful but sensitive, semiparabolic action. I know how it would have cast because I'd tried out the prototype a few months before, both around home and on a trip to Montana.

Actually, it had the kind of casting action I'd have told you I didn't much care for. Most of the fly rods I've tried that had the word parabolic anywhere in their descriptions just didn't seem quite right to me. Since I don't build rods and am not an authority on them, it's hard enough for me to describe what's *right* with a rod, let alone what's wrong. So let's just say there are certain perfectly respectable rod actions that are too demanding for me or that I just plain don't understand.

I tried out the Maurer prototype in the driveway, and for the first five minutes it didn't work so well. Then I got the hang of it, and it worked beautifully. There is, after all, something about an especially fine rod that will educate a caster if he's at least marginally competent and not completely brain dead.

I had a thing for this rod because it had spoken to me, and because the one that had been in the now-empty shipping tube was serial number 001 of a model George calls The Trout Bum, an allusion to some old fishing book.

So I stood on the porch, looking down into the empty tube, and after those few initial moments of disbelief, my first rational thought was, This was bound to happen.

I mean it. For more than twenty years now I've been shipping fly rods back and forth to be repaired or refinished, buying and selling them through the mail and lugging them around in cars and on airplanes, and in all that time I'd never lost one. And I know it happens, I've heard all the horror stories. Now and then it would occur to me that I was living on borrowed time, but what do you do with information like that? When you're lucky, all you can do is accept it graciously and forge ahead.

Now I don't mean to say I'm careless. I'm as careful as I can be with my rods, but it's real life and there are perils.

Along with most of the other fishermen I know, I've left spare rods in unattended vehicles for long periods of time; vehicles parked, sometimes for days on end, in secluded spots, where a villain could take all the time and make all the noise he wanted to breaking in.

Sure, I've considered the risk, but you've gotta have a spare, right? And it should be a good rod, too, because if you end up needing it you don't want to spend the rest of the trip fishing with a club. That would only make you feel worse about the one you broke.

In fact, the only time I ever broke a rod on the water was on one of the rare days when I *hadn't* brought a spare. I felt like an idiot. One of the guys I was with had an extra rod, but I don't want to tell you what I had to go through to get it from him. I've often wondered why so many of my friends have a cruel streak. He said, "Now be careful with it," which he thought was pretty damn funny.

I never used to worry too much about spare rods because my old pickup—a Ford so elderly it had been dropped from the Blue Book—always looked like the least likely vehicle in any parking lot to have anything valuable in it: the perfect camouflage. Now I have a new truck—or, I should say, a newer old truck—that actually looks pretty spiffy. Right after I got it I passed a friend on a county road.

I honked and waved, but he just gave me a blank look. Later he said, "Oh, that was you. I thought some yuppie stole your hat."

If the stories you hear can be believed—and there's no reason why they can't—more rods are lost on commercial airlines than anywhere else. Sometimes your luggage just vanishes temporarily, only to turn up a day or two later. The airline is usually happy to drop it off at the hotel for you, but that doesn't help people like us because we're not *at* the hotel. We're two more flights and a boat ride away, trying like hell to borrow a rod.

Another thing that can happen is, you arrive in British Columbia or wherever with empty rod cases. That's the standard trick, they say: steal the rods and send the cases on to their destination to cover your tracks. They say you should open your rod tubes and check inside every time you get your hands on them. That's probably a good idea, but, honestly, how useful would it be to know, when your flight leaves in ten minutes, that your four favorite fly rods are now in the possession of an anonymous slimy bastard somewhere in, say, Vancouver?

The only way to be absolutely sure is to take your rods on board with you. This is problematic with those long, two-piece-rod cases, but I have managed it a time or two, usually on short flights from Denver to Montana. The trick is to insist to everyone right up to the supervisor that the rods absolutely must stay with you, constantly pointing out that rod cases are no longer than a topcoat and that there is a closet on every commercial jet tall enough to hang a topcoat in, right?

All you have to do is get someone to admit, "Well, yes,

I suppose that's true . . ." and then keep pushing, avoiding rudeness if possible, but not forgetting that you're the customer, without whom this android who's currently busting your chops wouldn't even have a job.

Once someone breaks down and says okay, use their name at every roadblock: "Ms. So-and-so upstairs said it would be all right." As long as it was someone else's decision, they'll usually let you through.

But all this takes superhuman persistence, and you have to be a good whiner, so I can't *always* make it work.

The only time an airline ever lost my rods, it happened on the return trip. They showed up a day later, and a guy from United Airlines drove the 50 miles or so from Denver to deliver them to my door and apologize for the inconvenience. It had even been an understandable screwup.

I remember dashing to the United counter in Vancouver with my partner, just minutes before our plane left, and panting, "Our Wilderness Airlines flight was late."

The guy said, "What else is new?"

He also said we might have to live with the fact that our duffels and rod cases would take a later flight to Denver. I didn't like the sound of that, but there didn't seem to be anything to do about it. We could have waited for a later flight ourselves, but then our stuff could have arrived ahead of us.

Sure enough, we got into Denver at about two in the morning and learned that our luggage was probably in either Vancouver or Seattle. The woman at the baggage counter said they'd deliver it to us as soon as it came in.

That seemed okay to me, but my partner was cursing, pacing, sputtering something about suing the airline and kicking those pastel-colored plastic chairs. It was late at night and the airport was nearly empty. The sound of chairs being kicked echoed down the vacant corridors. In the far distance a guy pushing a broom stopped and looked to see what all the commotion was about.

"Look," I said, "this is a drag, but why don't we just get in your car, go home and get some sleep?"

"We can't do that," he said.

"Why not?"

"Because my car keys are in my goddamn duffel bag, that's why!"

When I went to Alaska, I tried something some friends had told me about. I shipped a trunk full of gear and a pad-locked case full of rods to a friend's house in Anchorage— second-day express, heavily insured. That was expensive, but I liked it. My friend called before I left to say that my stuff was safe in his garage, so all I had to do was breeze through the airport with a newspaper under my arm, not worrying about how I was going to catch fish if my gear went to Tibet. I could direct all my attention to the possibility of dying in a horrible plane crash.

So I've been careful and I do insure the rods now, even though that bothers me, because when you insure something you're betting against yourself, which probably isn't healthy. Still, it's a way of negotiating the paradox of wanting to own fine fishing tackle but *not* wanting to be ruled by material possessions. The best solution seems to be to buy the best stuff I can afford (or not afford, as the case may be) and then use it hard and otherwise put it in harm's way with a fatalistic shrug.

And okay, insure the stuff, too, although that may not

necessarily mean what you think it means. As the insurance agent said, "People think I sell security, but I don't. There *is* no security."

For a while I carried the biggest, sturdiest rod case I could find. It was made of some kind of high-impact plastic, padded inside with foam, with a good, solid handle, four latches and two hasps for padlocks. It held as many as five standard rod tubes, plus a couple of reels.

If you thought about it for a minute, you'd have realized it was too long and skinny to be a gun case, but it did have that look about it, and I spent a lot of time explaining to baggage and security types that it held rods instead of firearms.

I lugged this thing to Scotland and back one summer and I was thinking of stopping in London to get a can of spray paint so I could write FLY RODS—NOT GUNS down both sides of it.

In Boston on the return trip, I dragged myself up to the baggage counter and flopped the case on the scale. I'd been up for twenty-some hours, and the strong coffee they serve on Virgin Atlantic was beginning to wear off. The woman behind the counter looked as bad as I did: tired and harried, as though she'd been on duty for three days straight. She looked at the case and asked, "Is that shotguns?"

"No, fly rods," I said.

"Are they loaded?" she asked.

"No," I said truthfully, "they are not loaded."

"Okay," she said, "have a nice flight."

I didn't catch a salmon on that trip, but I flew I don't know how many thousands of miles on seven separate flights through three countries and twelve time zones and still had my rods when I got home. It was a small but meaningful victory.

I once actually spent a week on the phone calling every airline I was ever likely to take, plus the FAA in Washington, D.C., trying to find out how short a rod case I'd have to have to be able to carry the rods on board any commercial flight. You'd think that would be carved in marble somewhere (hence the call to Washington) but it's not. Every airline makes its own baggage regulations, and, judging from the people I talked to, the actual rules are either unknown or none of your business, which means there's probably no absolute guarantee against hearing those dreaded words, "You're gonna have to check that."

The best I could do was learn that a 36-inch case will fit in the overhead bins on the *majority* of commercial planes. That translates into, at a bare minimum, a brace of three-piece, 8-foot rods. Of course most of the big airliners travel between major cities, and a fisherman's destination is usually as far from a city as he can get.

I'll admit to being a tackle freak, but I wasn't anxious to replace all my favorite two-piece rods with new three-piece models. If I was going on a trip, I figured I was headed for a place where the fishing is pretty good, so naturally I wanted to use my best rods. I thoroughly enjoy good fishing tackle until the moment I have to check it as luggage. Then I wish I used garage-sale fiberglass rods and plastic reels.

But I did finally break down—when it comes to fly rods, I *always* break down—and I figured the only way to avoid pining away for my favorite two-piece sticks on a trip was to get equally fine three-piece rods. So I had Mike

Clark build me an 8 foot, 6/7 weight with darkly flamed cane and a little detachable, 2-inch fighting butt. Then, within weeks, I got a lovely old Leonard Model 50-H with a Coke-bottle grip and intermediate wraps that had been flawlessly restored by John Bradford in Fort Worth, Texas. They're both such sweet rods I couldn't tell you which is the backup.

I already had some lighter, 4- and 5-weight three-piece rods, but I still had to get a stubby little hard case with a carrying strap that would hold no fewer than four rods in their bags.

It was a shocking example of what a friend calls "retail therapy," but I've found that if you have a certain kind of inner peace (and no kids) you can buy things you want but can't afford and feel okay about it.

So I've been careful and lucky, as I said, and it was probably inevitable that I would lose a rod sooner or later, if only because it's rare to have so much fun without paying some kind of dues. That fly rod that disappeared somewhere between Pennsylvania and Colorado was insured, and George Maurer made me another one—Trout Bum serial number 001-A—so I suppose it turned out okay.

I was a little put out that the company that shipped it, against my objections, insisted on declaring it "lost" instead of "stolen." I pointed out that the shipping tube had been sliced open neatly and that we were talking about a 50-inch brown anodized aluminum tube with a brass cap, not the kind of thing that disappears by rolling under a desk.

I do have the Gierach family temper, but in cooler moments I can usually manage to become philosophical. Things like this happen; it could have been worse, and so on.

Then again, it's a moral universe and some people just don't deserve to be forgiven. Like, for instance, Adolf Hitler, Saddam Hussein and the son of a bitch who stole my rod.

CHAPTER

7

Fly-Caster's Elbow

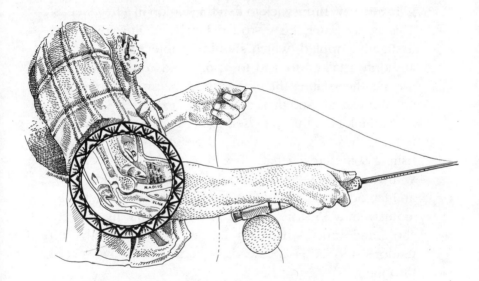

I'm sitting at my desk with the front door open so I can hear the hissing of the camp stove out in the yard. It's running on a nearly empty can of propane left over from the last camping trip, and when the hissing stops, it'll be time to go screw in a fresh one and re-light the low flame under the pot.

I'm slowly boiling the head of a blue grouse to get the skull for my modest skull collection, and this has to be done outside because it stinks with some authority. You'd think it would smell something like grouse stock for soup, but it doesn't. Probably something to do with the feathers.

It's a bright, crisp fall day in Colorado—the kind that makes visitors want to chuck everything and move here—and I'm typing with a big ice pack Ace-bandaged halfway down my right arm. The plastic bag I put the ice in is leaking slightly, so there's a small puddle of water on the floor next to the desk.

I have a lingering case of fly-caster's elbow, and I'm going to New Brunswick to fish for salmon in a few weeks. This is big-water, heavy-rod fishing, and I'm going into it slightly crippled, which should be interesting. The last authority I talked to said to apply cold compresses after casting, then slather the elbow and forearm with arnica oil and apply heat. And then do the wrist exercises.

I think I did this to myself in Texas back in April while fighting those big ol' bass on a 9-weight fly rod. We were fishing some tanks (that's Texan for "ponds") so choked with weeds that when you hooked a fish you couldn't give an inch or the bass would be lost forever in the vegetation, along with a $5 store-bought bass fly. So the fights were short and brutal—hard on tackle and, apparently, on tendons, too. After a few days of it, the elbow started throbbing.

I ignored it, which is usually the best thing to do with aches and pains. I finished the Texas trip and fished through the month of May around home, telling myself I wasn't getting old or anything; that, in fact, young, nimble athletes in their twenties get injured all the time, so much so that you need a medical degree to fully understand the sports page.

By the time Ed and I did a tour of some rivers in Montana in June, the elbow was sore enough that I couldn't straighten it out quickly with that slight but powerful snap you need for long casts. I compensated by stopping the forward cast a little short, hauling the line a little harder than normal with my left hand and lowering the rod tip by dropping my shoulder.

It worked great.

Actually, it worked surprisingly well, considering.

Actually, it hardly worked at all and, in a sport where form is appreciated, it looked like hell, too. But I caught some fish.

So when I got home I went to a doctor, which was a daring and desperate move. I have nothing against the established medical profession except that when you visit an M.D. there's always the chance you'll come home broke and/or dead.

The doc told me that casting a fly rod and swinging a tennis racket were both unnatural motions that could easily cause this kind of tendon injury. Something to do with the distribution of the load and the sudden starts and stops. He's probably right about tennis, but fly casting? Unnatural? I'd already decided the guy was a quack before he told me to "curtail my activities for a while"—in the middle of fishing season.

I thought of saying, "Look, I'm an outdoor writer. If I 'curtail my activities,' I won't be able to pay you," but I thought of that after I got home, which was too late.

I tried to learn how to fly-cast left-handed, which is something I should be able to do since I was left-handed until I was about six years old. I got polio then, and my left side was paralyzed for a while. By necessity, I did everything right-handed, and when I came out of it, I had *become* right-handed, although no one noticed until I went back to school and turned in a writing assignment that was back-

wards. I mean it was written from right to left with all the
letters neatly reversed so you could read it in a mirror.

They thought I was just screwing around until one of
my teachers tried it and realized it was pretty difficult to
pull off. I was a joker, but I was also known to be lazy, and
she didn't think I'd work that hard just for a laugh. She had
me write something while she watched. She asked my
folks, "Wasn't he left-handed before?" They both talked to
some doctors, and so on. Then she actually apologized for
yelling at me.

I eventually did learn to write legibly, although for
years any time I printed something, a few random letters
would always be facing the wrong way.

That was a little over forty years ago, but I thought
there must still be some old neural pathways left that would
let me cast with my left hand. It was pretty awkward at first,
but after a little practice I got to where I could make a
decent, short-range cast left-handed. But that was about it.
I couldn't do anything fancy and couldn't get any distance
because, although I could make the left hand and arm cast,
I couldn't make the right hand haul the line.

I guess it had been too long; I just couldn't make the
brain switch back to the left side again. On a lawn, where
I could think about it, I could cast okay left-handed, but
on the water, with the thoughtlessness caused by fish and
current, I just put the damned rod in my right hand and
gutted it out.

I limped through a few more weeks of trout fishing
and then consulted Dr. Pao, an acupuncturist, on the advice of a friend who said, "I've seen people limp in there
and dance out." I'd never been to an acupuncturist, but it
wasn't because of the witch-doctor paranoia some Americans have about them. The fact is, they were curing people

(or at least doing them no harm) back when our guys were still bleeding their patients with leeches.

The woman at the front desk said, "First time, huh? Are you nervous?"

"No!" I said.

"Good," she said. "It not hurt as much if you're relaxed."

"That's helpful," I said.

When I met the doctor, I said, "It's tendinitis."

" 'Tendinitis' just a label," Pao said. "This is your very own sore elbow. How did you do this? Tennis?"

He pulled and twisted my arm until we had determined exactly where it hurt and how much, which by then was a lot. Then he stuck pins in it, toasted it with a burning bundle of herbs that looked like a cigar and smelled like a boiling grouse head, and he gave me some herbs to drink three times a day that tasted like . . . I don't know. There's no comparison. The principle in operation here was pretty obvious: If you have the guts to drink this stuff repeatedly, you have the inner strength to cure yourself.

I didn't quite dance out the door of the place, but it helped a lot. Two weeks later I was almost completely well —just an odd twinge in the elbow now and then—but then I went to Scotland for salmon and then to Alaska for salmon, trout, char and grayling and managed to spring the elbow again. And you thought being an outdoor writer was all fun.

Fly-caster's elbow is a terrible malady because you can't get any sympathy. People say things like, "You hurt your elbow fishing? I haven't been fishing in two months." Those who do fish a lot indirectly question your manhood, pointedly saying things like, "Well, I never hurt *my* elbow . . ." And of course techno-freaks preen: "If you'd use modern graphite rods instead of those old bamboos, that wouldn't happen."

Friends trying to be helpful sometimes can't resist attempts at humor: "I knew a guy who got that. Had to give up fishing. Finally lost the arm." That's the kind of thing you say to stop someone from whining. I didn't think I was whining, but sometimes I might have been and just didn't remember doing it.

Then again, A.K., who's a professional fly tier, once got tendonitis from tying too many flies too fast for too long, and people felt sorry for *him*.

So I grudgingly curtailed my activities a little bit, sticking with lighter fly rods, narrower streams and using the canoe on lakes to avoid long casts. It didn't get any worse, and it might actually have gotten a little better.

Then I went to a great brook trout lake where fish were rising like crazy, but the wind was blowing too hard to float the canoe. I made long casts into the wind all day, caught lots of trout and had a pretty sore elbow by the time I got home.

Then grouse season opened and I found that I had a little trouble smartly mounting the shotgun, which is why there's only one grouse head boiling out in the yard. I was going to make another skull mount for Ed, but at least I have an excuse for missing that second bird.

Okay, so maybe this isn't the kind of thing that forces you to confront your mortality or anything, but it does get you to thinking about basic mechanics.

I went to a therapist who used ultrasound, massage and herbal ointments (but no needles) and gave me a tennis elbow brace: a device that fits below the elbow on the forearm to hold the tendon in place.

The thing had a familiar look to it—simultaneously sterile and mechanical—and when I got home I peeked into that bottom dresser drawer in the bedroom where I keep all my old Ace bandages, heating pads and plastic vials, each containing a few leftover painkillers. Plus, of course, the knee, wrist and ankle braces, some of which date back to the days when they used metal for the stiffen ers instead of hard plastic.

For some reason it was comforting to be reminded that I've been banging up my joints since I was about eighteen, both at work and at play. I saved the stuff thinking I might need it again sometime, although I somehow always manage to injure something new, which naturally requires a different gadget. It won't be much longer before I have the equipment to immobilize every part of my body that's supposed to bend.

So, now that I think about it, I guess I've always had this tendency to push a little too hard in most ways, pulling in my horns only after I got hurt. That's why I have a few scars and sore spots—physical and otherwise—which are probably a fair price to pay to learn how things work. That's also why Dad used to say I was reckless. Maybe I was, but after years of testing I've developed a pretty good sense of where the boundaries are. Naturally, they're a little farther out than you might think.

The elbow is actually much better now, considering that the real cure would have been to take a year off from fishing. The ice packs, ointments and exercises help, the brace lets me keep on casting, and there's only one more big fishing trip this season. Then there will be some smaller ones, then it'll be winter and maybe I *can* actually curtail my activities for a while. Maybe I'll get a bunch of flies tied. A.K. told me you can tie flies with tendonitis as long as you prop your elbow up on a stack of books.

I haven't been fishing in eight days now, but I tried casting the salmon rod this morning and the elbow was fine —really—just a slight twinge. The rod is a 9½-foot, 8-weight bamboo with a 5-inch fighting butt, and I suppose a lighter one would be better, but I've already spent the price of a graphite salmon rod on doctors, and I don't care that much for graphite anyway.

So the old rod will do and so will the old elbow. The last doctor said it's not even serious enough for drugs now, which is just as well. I'd hate to catch a huge salmon in New Brunswick, only to have my friends say, "Yeah, but I hear he was on steroids."

8

Salmon

I guess I decided to try fly-fishing for Atlantic salmon out of a feeling of envy. From a distance it doesn't seem to make much sense—fishing for a fish that's not supposed to bite and, sure enough, usually doesn't—but the people who do it swear by it, and that makes you wonder what *they* know that *you* don't.

Apparently, it's an acquired taste, which is something I understand. For instance, like most young men in America at the time, I learned to like beer in my late teens, but if I think back far enough, I can remember a time when it tasted so awful I thought, So this is one of the great pleasures of adulthood. Jeez . . . On the other hand—and maybe more to the point—I never did get into caviar because I couldn't afford the breaking-in period.

I've been Atlantic salmon fishing twice now and I've learned this much: Salmon fishers brag more loudly about their many failures than about their few successes, not only because there are more of them, but because it's believed that enduring failure builds character. But then they also greet success as if they deserved it based on the flip side of the same premise. Namely, that living graciously with your defeats gives you the right to celebrate the occasional victory without false modesty.

These fantastic stories of days when salmon were actually caught are wonderful. The lodge grows quiet, everyone scoots forward on their chairs to listen, wide-eyed and gullible. Of course the guy's telling the truth. A real salmon fisher would no sooner lie about this than snag fish with a jig.

Before I went salmon fishing, every salmon fisher I know and every book I read said the same thing: There's a good chance you won't catch one. In fact, since salmon don't eat when they run out of the sea and into the rivers to spawn, catching one is almost an accident. Almost. There *is* a reason why the odd salmon will bite a certain fly on a certain day, it's just that no one seems to know what that reason is.

That doesn't stop the big volumes from coming, though. One thing I've noticed about fly-fishing writers is, the less sure they are of their subject, the fatter their books get.

I *have* been told by some old-timers that, although catching an Atlantic salmon on a fly has always been a ticklish business, it wasn't always as unlikely as it is now. That's because there used to be lots more fish, so even though it was still maybe only one salmon in a hundred that was dumb enough or confused enough to bite a fly, the odds were a hell of a lot better.

One guy I talked to went so far as to say that at a lot of the places where you fish for salmon now—sometimes paying a hell of a lot of money for the privilege—there just aren't any fish, or at least not enough to be worth the effort. He seemed to be implying that, in some cases at least, all that stuff about the Mystery and the Experience, although once true enough, was now more like a scam.

All I know for sure is, the few Atlantic salmon fishers I'm acquainted with like it a lot and do now and then catch some fish, but they get a little vague when you question them carefully about the actual quality of the fishing, while the majority of my friends see it as the sport of kings and— since they're not kings and don't want to be—they pretty much ignore it.

So I went to the Beauly River in Scotland and got skunked. I had the rhetoric of the sport firmly in mind, but I still couldn't believe it. ("Oh, believe it," said one of the ghillies.) Of course I'd heard this described. You go some- where far away—preferably to a river with ghillies and castles along its banks—cast methodically for six days with pretty flies and then go home. If you don't have stories like that, you're not a real salmon fisher.

Thank God, four out of the five of us on the Beauly that week went fishless, and the other guy got only one. That's one of the undeniable characteristics of fishing: get- ting skunked is less painful the more company you have. I did begin to understand why traditional Atlantic salmon flies are so complicated, though. On about the fourth fish- less day you begin to think, maybe if I had more stuff on my hook . . .

That was in June. In October of the same year I was at the Nepisiguit River Camp in New Brunswick for the short, four-day week that closes the season there. I was the odd guy in a party of six, most of whom were much older and all of whom had a lot more salmon fishing under their belts.

Many salmon fishers are older folks, at least in part because it can be an expensive sport and it's mostly older people who can afford it. Maybe there's also something about maturity that breeds the necessary patience. Or is it fatalism? Anyway, there's some wisdom to be picked up here, and at the age of forty-something, with some blond hair still left in my beard, I could be referred to as "the young, skinny guy."

Some of these men had fished together for a long time and had some procedures worked out among them. For instance, one of the guys had bad legs and couldn't wade, so a couple of his friends, and maybe a guide, would haul him out to a good spot, prop him against a rock and leave him to fish. When it was time for him to move or relieve himself, they'd haul him back to shore—without any wisecracks.

When I was introduced to the man known as the Doc, he shook my hand and said, "You look like a flaming, bearded liberal."

"That's correct," I said, "and you strike me as one of those square-jawed conservatives."

"Well," he said, "let's just stick to fishing, then."

Which we did for a change. I do have some political opinions, and I'm usually not shy about sharing them, but getting into an ideological brawl in a fishing camp is like having an affair with a married woman in a small town: It can be worth the trouble, but there are still lots of reasons to avoid it.

I found these guys—the Doc included—to be generous; more generous, I have to say, than your average Rocky Mountain trout fishermen. They coached me as well as they could, considering that the ultimate secret to success is pretty much unknown. There are smaller, more mundane secrets, however.

For instance, in the spring the salmons' mouths are soft, so you don't want to strike when you get a hit. Just the drag of the line against the reel, they say, is enough to sink the hook. But by September and October, the salmons' mouths have grown as hard as dry wall—yet another of the amazing changes these fish go through—so "you want to *hammer* them." You also want to sharpen your hooks to needle points. They said the problem in the fall is that many more fish are hooked than landed and, as always, damned few are hooked.

There were at least two items of tackle these guys all had in common: *very* good reels (including several Bogdans) and professional-quality hook hones.

Fly selection, as usual, was open to discussion, but the preferred local theory called for streamers. Ken Gray, owner of the lodge, explained this in some detail. It seems that in the fall, when the hen salmon are getting ready to spawn, the male fish get particularly aggressive toward the parr. Salmon parr are only a few inches long at best, but they can still fertilize eggs, so the males like to chase them out of the pools. Knowing this, you fish a streamer to imitate a little fish, and if that doesn't work, you try something else, and then something else, and then come back to the streamer again because something (who knows what?) might have changed in the last hour or so.

Ken was different from the Scottish ghillies in any number of ways. Most notably, he seemed to think Atlantic salmon could actually be caught, even by me. He's also the fourth generation of his family to live and fish on that stretch of the Nepisiguit, so his knowledge of it is now almost genetic.

Fall is supposed to be a good time. There are plenty of salmon in the river (at least by modern standards), the water is cool but not too cold, skies are often overcast and sometimes there's enough rain to raise the river a little and get the fish moving. No one can tell you exactly why a salmon bites—*if* he bites—but experience has at least shown what the best conditions are.

The group at the camp the week before had had it all —clouds, rain, rising water—and they'd caught fish. I forget how many now, but it was an enviable number. There were lots more strikes than fish landed, and you could actually look that up in the camp log book. I think salmon fishers count strikes if only to be counting *something*.

Naturally, by the time we arrived the sky had turned bright blue and the water had dropped and cleared and cooled considerably. Everyone agreed that it didn't look good, although, of course, one never really knows.

In four days, fishing the camp's private pools as well as some public water upstream, one guy got blanked, the rest of us each landed a couple of grilse, and one guy also landed a salmon of about 17 pounds, all pretty much against the odds.

One morning I had a salmon on long enough to get him on the reel before the fly came loose. The hook had been sharpened to surgical specifications, and I'd set up hard, though apparently not hard enough. Ken, who'd watched the whole thing from a high bank, said the fish would have gone about 15 pounds. This was generally considered to be not bad—though less than great—Atlantic salmon fishing.

•

The distinction between a grilse and a salmon is something I'm still getting used to. In one sense, a grilse is just a small salmon, a fish around 25 inches in length that's spent one winter feeding at sea. A salmon is the same fish after two or more winters at sea, but those subsequent winters make all the difference.

To a trout fisherman, a 25-inch grilse weighing several pounds is a hell of a nice fish, and even on a stout, 8-weight rod, a big one will really take you for a ride. Okay, but if it survives and returns the following year, it'll be a by-God salmon weighing 10 or 12 pounds. If it survives even more seasons (the probability declines severely with time) it'll weigh maybe 25 or 30 pounds, and then maybe 40, and so on.

What this means to a duffer like me is, you can catch all the grilse you want and be happy as a clam, but you haven't caught a salmon until you've caught a salmon.

I liked it. I even sort of liked it in Scotland in a masochistic sort of way, and when I said that out loud, someone replied, "Ah, you poor lad." But of course New Brunswick was better. I haven't acquired the rarefied sensibilities of the true Atlantic salmon angler, but I do understand that catching fish is preferable to not catching fish.

After two trips and a few fish, I'm beginning to get a vague idea of where salmon lie in a stream, and the fact that they bite best in cloudy weather with certain water temperatures makes them a little more like big trout and therefore more recognizable.

Before you actually do it, Atlantic salmon fishing

seems terribly classy, elite, even snobbish, and that worried me a little. I don't have any business being a snob and I don't think anyone else does, either. But then when you're out there on the water you find that it's just fishing. You know, eat breakfast, string up a rod and wade into the river. You have to learn to live with the unlikelihood of catching anything, but that's really pretty easy: You simply think, This is how it is. It's not like I could be doing it better.

Well, you actually *could* be doing it better, but maybe it wouldn't make a difference.

I've even begun to like some fly patterns better than others for reasons other than that they're just pretty. Like the Herb Johnson Special. I had six or seven strikes and actually landed a fish on that fly—the regional full-dress streamer pattern, with a silver tinsel tag; silver-ribbed black wool body; long, white bucktail throat under a shorter blue hackle; mixed natural, yellow and purple bucktail wing and jungle cock eyes.

In the weeks before that trip I'd pored through some books looking for local patterns and had found only one: the Nepisiguit Gray. It's a handsome, traditional salmon wet-fly pattern, a little on the drab side with its grizzly hackle, gray wool body and bronze mallard wing, but it still has the regulation tip, tag, butt, golden pheasant tail and such—all those bangles that seem unnecessary, even as you're faithfully reproducing the pattern exactly as it's described in the book. I mean, if it didn't mean something, they wouldn't go to all this trouble, would they?

I tied up a handful of them, but when I showed them to one of the guides he said they were nice, but the pattern hadn't actually been fished there "in about a hundred years." Pointing to the other side of the fly box where the streamers I'd just bought were laid out—the Montreals,

Undertakers and good old Herb Johnson Specials—he said, "These are what you'll be using."

So I'm slowly learning, although some important questions still remain. For instance, who is Herb Johnson?

If you ever decide to do this, you *must* read a book on the Atlantic salmon's life cycle first. I won't try to rush through it here because, in human terms, there's just too much starvation, hardship and what you'd have to call heroism to cram into a few paragraphs. But I think you have to know about it because then, although you really want to catch a fish and you try as hard as you can to do it, there will be a small part of you that's happy to see them get away.

I think that's where that gesture comes from; the one Canadian salmon guides do so well when you miss a strike or when a fish throws the hook. It's a lopsided shrug that I take to mean, "Life is ironic, ey?"

CHAPTER

9

Grayling

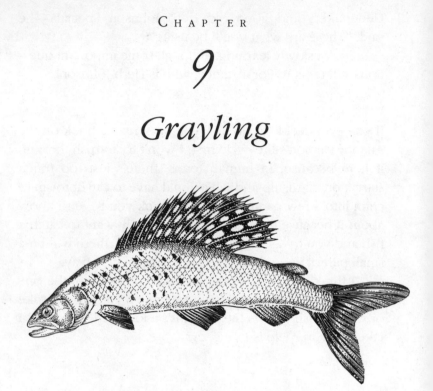

*H*ave you ever noticed that grayling always get
listed last? Below silver, sockeye and king salmon, rainbow
trout and char in Alaska; under lake trout and pike in the
Northwest Territories; as an afterthought on the Big Hole
River in Montana; as a footnote to the high mountain lakes
of Utah, Wyoming and Colorado. I don't know how many
full-color brochures I've read that say something to the
effect that "if there's nothing else happening, you can always fool around with the grayling."

When Ed came back from a fly-fishing trip to Austria a
few years ago, I asked him how grayling were viewed over

there, hoping for a little Central European enlightenment. "They think they're a trash fish," he said. "Face it, grayling are a neat fish that nobody likes."

Well maybe, but there are exceptions. For instance, I like grayling—always have—and I've met plenty of other fishermen who do too, although perhaps not enough to constitute a real movement.

Mike Schmetzer, a man I met in Alaska a few years ago, likes grayling a lot and seeks them out, but then he's an unusual case because he likes to fish with dry flies and bamboo rods. Nothing against Alaskan fly-fishing—it's a lot of fun, especially if you like bears—but you have to admit that most of it is not what you'd call delicate. Many of the Alaskan fly fishers I met used 8- and 9-weight rods and carried their 7 pounds of split shot on the hip opposite their .44 Magnums so they wouldn't walk lopsided.

More to the point, maybe if you catch enough king salmon the size of small antelope or silvers that smoke your high-tech reels, you begin to lose interest in pretty little $2\frac{1}{2}$-pound grayling.

A.K. and our mutual friend Koke Winter also like grayling, although I've never known either of them to go far out of their way to catch them.

Once we were floating the Madison River in Montana in Koke's antique aluminum johnboat, the one that looks like it was used as cover in a gunfight. It was late in the day and we were down in the channels above Ennis Lake when A.K. hooked a fish, played it for a few seconds with a puzzled look on his face and said, "You know, I think this is a grayling."

"No it's not," Koke said, leaning on the oars and gazing downstream.

"Well," A.K. said, "actually, I think it is."

"You've caught a whitefish," Koke said.

A.K. netted the fish and held it 3 inches from Koke's nose. Koke said, "Son of a bitch! That's a grayling!" and pulled hard for shore.

That's what you do, of course, because grayling are a schooling fish. Where there's one, there's more. Casting from the bank, we caught grayling until well after dark, admiring each one in the failing light and saying things like, "Koke, there's something wrong with this whitefish. Look at this big fin."

Getting into those fish was such a milestone that now, when trying to remember when something happened in Montana, we mark it as so many years before or after we caught all those grayling on the Madison. But when we tell the story, most listeners say, "Oh . . . But did you get any *trout?*"

The first grayling I ever caught were in some remote, pretty mountain lakes and beaver ponds in the Colorado Rockies. We've had small populations of grayling here since they were first introduced way back in 1899. The biologists say they do okay at high altitudes, where the water doesn't get too warm for them, but they've never really caught on with local fishermen, many of whom still think they're some kind of sucker.

It's hard to believe anyone actually makes that mistake. A grayling is a quick, roughly trout-shaped fish with a deeply forked tail and a mouth right in the front of the face where it should be. Of course the distinguishing feature is the tall dorsal fin that looks like an ornate sail. This fin is used in mating displays, so it's larger on the males, but it's still plenty big on the females.

I've caught grayling in several lakes and ponds in Colorado, the Madison and Big Hole Rivers in Montana, stretches of the Kazan and First Island Rivers in the North-west Territories and the Agulowak in Alaska. In my color slides the fish are anywhere from iridescent grayish silver to bluish purple to bronze, always with those sparse V- or check-shaped black spots clustered toward the front of the body. The larger, oval spots on the dorsal fin are blue to bluish green, and the fin margin is anywhere from pale blue to a delicate pink. The tail, pectoral and anal fins are usually a dusky bluish yellow, and the pelvic fins have cream or pink stripes.

Anyone who honestly thinks this is a sucker shouldn't be trusted with sharp objects like fish hooks.

Grayling do school up in both lakes and streams, so although they're not always a snap to locate, once you've found them, you've found them, at least for a while. In flowing water they like pools and the slack water on the insides of bends. In lakes they cruise, often very close to shore, especially in the mornings and evenings.

It can be misleading to characterize an entire species of fish, but the ones I've caught do live up to the traditional profile. For one thing, they're "aggressive to the surface," as they say. That is, they'll often rise nicely to dry flies even when there are no bugs on the water. I have fond memories of big grayling on the Kazan River rocketing up through 4 feet of miraculously clear water to grab an Elk Hair Caddis, and of smaller ones in Colorado lakes swimming 3 feet out of their way to take a #16 Adams.

Then again, they'll sometimes get into what seems like a playful or curious mood and inspect, follow, swirl at and otherwise mess with three or four different fly patterns before deciding to take one. As Al McClane said, "You may come face to face with a grayling and be ignored; yet it will study every fly as though trying to help you find the right one."

Standard, boilerplate grayling lore says these fish prefer small, dark flies. That's true enough in my limited experience, and they do have smaller mouths than trout, so maybe they've evolved with a taste for little bugs. Still, you have to wonder how they'd act during a heavy Brown Drake or stonefly hatch.

The old story about grayling being hard to hook because they have soft mouths is flat wrong, but they do have the odd tendency to roll on a dry fly, coming half out of the water next to it and taking it on the way down. That makes most of us strike too soon, either missing the fish entirely or hooking it poorly. In typical human style, we like to think that's the fish's fault.

When fishing for grayling you come to understand the need for a slight but very real hesitation on the strike, which requires a sense of timing and nerves of steel.

Grayling are found in parts of Montana—where they're native—and they've been introduced into some mountain lakes in Wyoming, Utah and Colorado, where they form what guidebooks and biologists like to call "token populations." The once-native grayling of Michigan are now gone. The heart of the grayling's range is in Alaska and northern Canada, especially the Yukon and Northwest Territories where, all things being equal, they grow to their best size.

I guess one should mention that they're often the smallest game fish found in their home waters. A grayling approaching 3 pounds is big enough to mount, and the all-tackle world record is just shy of 6. But then they're also beautiful and real patsies for a dry fly and, after all, size isn't everything, right?

Scientists once thought there were three distinct species: the arctic, Montana and the extinct Michigan grayling.

Now it's believed that there is only one species in North America: the arctic grayling, *Thymallus arcticus*. Or at least that's how things stood the last time I did any reading on the subject.

For the record, grayling are delicious, but then the only ones I've ever eaten were at shore lunches, fresh by a matter of minutes in a situation where a stale granola bar tastes like venison coventry. Also for the record, I'm told they don't freeze well. One of the sad realities of fishing is, you cannot reproduce an authentic shore lunch at home, even if you prop the screen doors open so the mosquitos can get in.

I once had a grayling shore lunch on a stream that, as near as I can tell, had never been fished before. A friend and I were fishing from a camp in the Northwest Territories, and one night as we were going over a map of the area I pointed to a small stream a few miles up the lake from camp and asked the head guide what the fishing was like there. He said he didn't know because no one had ever fished it.

"*No one?*"

"Well, no white people, anyway, and probably no Indians, either, because they fish from boats with nets and that thing isn't even navigable."

None of the guides wanted to take us there. They said it would be a pain in the ass and, they assured us, the fish wouldn't be very big. But my partner and I weren't about to pass up a chance at virgin water, so we begged, then insisted and finally pulled out all the stops and hinted at an enormous tip.

That was some grand bullshitting on my part, because

at the time I had a plane ticket home and about twenty bucks Canadian to my name, so my share of the actual tip at the end of the trip wasn't what it should have been.

I'm not bragging about that. Actually, I'm pretty ashamed of it because it wasn't a cute little fisherman's fib but a real lie about money to a fellow working stiff. I only bring it up to illustrate how desperate I was to be the first fisherman to cast a dry fly on an absolutely unfished stream. I was almost nauseous from the potential romance of it.

The next morning we motored over to the creek mouth, towing a canoe that we then alternately portaged and paddled a few miles up the stream. There was a pod of grayling in every pool, and our guide was delighted to see that the best fish we caught went about a pound and a half, or at least a pound lighter than the grayling we'd been catching in the nearby Kazan River.

He couldn't understand why we were having so much fun. These guides were already puzzled that we'd spend so much time catching grayling on dry flies when we could have been dredging for 30-plus pound lake trout with jigs and Flatfish. When we started slapping each other on the back over *little* grayling, they probably reached the same conclusion that most fishing guides eventually come to: that the clients themselves are nuts, but there's nothing wrong with their money.

Interestingly enough, these perfectly wild fish were a bit leader shy—as all grayling are said to be—and they would eat small dark dry flies, but not big light ones. Then again, sometimes we'd wade into a pool and the fish would swim over like tame ducks to inspect our boots.

Actually, we didn't have a "shore" lunch. The banks of that stream were so thick in tangled willows and mosquitos that we set up the camp stove on a few dry rocks in the

middle of the stream and ate sitting in the water: baked
beans, thick slices of homemade bread, lukewarm beer and
grayling killed and cleaned *after* the grease was melted in
the pan.

Best meal I ever had. I used to think that hunger was
the best sauce, but now I know there's a better one: the
knowledge that you have just fished where no one has
fished before.

According to the map, that little stream ran on for a
few more miles to where it drained out of a chain of small
lakes that our guide said had also never been fished. "No
way to run a boat up in there, and all the lakes are too
small to land a floatplane on," he said. His best guess was
that the small lakes would be full of pike, while the slack
water in the flowing channels between them would be
packed with grayling. But then, of course, who knew?
Chances were slim that anyone had ever set foot there, let
alone cast a fly or stretched a net.

That's when I experienced one of those rare moments
of perfect clarity: a simple realization of exactly where I
was. I was sitting in the middle of a small, unknown grayling stream looking at a waterproof map that covered 3500-
some square miles of lakes, ponds, marshes and streams—
a tiny chunk of the Northwest Territories' 1,352,000 square
miles, most of which are covered by water, but seldom
enough water in one place to either take a boat across or
land a floatplane, and not enough land to walk more than
a couple of miles in any one direction. From the camp we
were staying at, you could crank up the outboard and
motor 70 miles up and down Snowbird Lake and, if you
had the guts and the time, several hundred miles down the
Kazan to Hudson Bay, but in terms of total area, that's
nothing.

As a perpetual tourist fisherman you can spend your

life stumbling past fundamental truths that, because of the single-mindedness of fishing and the brevity of your stay, you can never quite get a handle on. But when you do accidentally grasp one, it's amazing how neatly everything slips into place.

I waved my hand over the map and said to the guide, "You mean to say *most* of this has never been fished?"

"Hell," he said, "damn near *none* of it's been fished."

10

The Kindness of Strangers

*I*t had been a busy summer so far: lots of fishing (which I sometimes say is my job) with a little bit of frantic writing (which really *is* my job) wedged in between. When I got back from twelve days in Alaska, I found that I was still mentally exhausted from the work, but also refreshed and invigorated from the fishing, which left me sort of stuck in neutral: weary, but not exactly ready to rest.

I guess there was a little sleep deprivation in there, too. Summer days in Alaska are so long you can end up fishing for eighteen hours and sleeping four or five. You don't actually feel tired, but after a week or so you start walking into trees and forgetting your friends' names.

Anyway, that's how I was feeling—pleasantly bushed and a little disoriented—when A.K. called to see if I wanted to go over to the Frying Pan River. I said I should stay home and work, but he didn't want to know what I *should* do, he wanted to know if I was going fishing. I thought for a minute and said, "Yeah, okay."

You have to understand that this is the annual trip; a tradition. Every season, sometime in late July or early August, the Green Drake and Pale Morning Dun mayfly hatches overlap perfectly on the Pan, and A.K., Ed and I have been hitting that—or at least trying to—for quite a few years now.

We always set up a comfortable camp at Roy Palm's place—whatever bird dogs he has around at the moment move in with us as camp mascots—and we fish hard, but also manage to relax a little, too. After all, the Pale Morning Duns and Green Drakes keep banker's hours, so there's no reason to be on the water at dawn, and a leisurely breakfast in fishing camp—drinking a third cup of coffee while scratching a retriever behind the ears—is pleasant if only because it's so rare.

I've fished the Pan long enough now to have seen it change some. The hatches are a little different than they were a dozen years ago—heavier here, lighter there—and I've seen fish sizes and numbers go up and down, though never so far down that it wasn't still a great stream.

But the biggest change has been a kind of gentrification. There are more houses along the river now, and most of the new ones are palatial numbers (rumored to have cost millions) with commanding views, lots of glass and, in the foreground, along the river, NO FISHING signs.

This is something I hate to see on general principles, and the first question that comes to mind when I come upon one of these huge, overbearing monstrosities of a house is, Who the hell do those people think they are? If it turns out that there's an afterlife, the owners of these things are going to have to account for having taken up a lot more than their fair share of room.

Then again, it *is* good for the environment, as holders of private water are always quick to point out. "A trout stream is better off being fished by a select few than being hammered by the mob," they say. As a dues-paying member of the mob, I've never liked the sanctimonious sound of that, and those who use it as an argument don't seem to realize how flimsy it sounds. As a friend of mine says, "If I'll never get to fish it, why the hell should I care how good it is?"

On the other hand, the three of us have fished the Frying Pan long enough to have some loose connections over there, so we can occasionally get on some of that private water. Sometimes we're invited out of the blue, so we don't even have to suck up. We do it when the chance comes along because, well, who wouldn't? But it sometimes makes me feel funny.

On this last trip, A.K. and I got on an especially good private stretch. Ed had already left, and it was my last day there—I really did have to get some work done—but A.K. would be staying on for a few more days to camp and fish by himself, which he likes to do. I knew he'd call me when he got back, just to let me know how great it had been after I left.

We drove up to our benefactor's house, past a sign that read, NO FISHING, DON'T EVEN ASK, and got a couple of big orange buttons to wear on our vests so that whoever needed to know (hired thugs? snipers?) could tell at a distance that we were legitimate guests of one of the landowners controlling that stretch of river.

I don't know if it was the haughty language of the sign or the big, gaudy buttons, but although the fishing was good with a Green Drake dry fly and an emerger on a short dropper, I didn't feel quite right about being there. This is not a new feeling for me, and it's never a simple or even a predictable one. It just pops up now and then to bother me. To be honest, though, it often conveniently bothers me on the drive home, after I've caught a bunch of big, private fish.

But not always. Sometimes when I'm fishing private water I see it as what it probably is—an example of the kindness of strangers—and I just enjoy it. When I pay a rod fee, I usually experience the righteousness of the capitalist: Maybe the fishing is better than on public water and maybe it's not, but by God I purchased the right to be there.

But then there are other times when I feel . . . well, if not actually guilty, then at least embarrassed, hoping no one I know sees me fishing behind the Keep Out sign or recognizes my truck parked up at the Big House. Sometimes I'll try to think of what I'm doing as a populist raid on the ruling class: After all, it may be a private stretch of river, but these are still the People's trout. Other times I'll amuse myself by planning to fish the place *without* permission: figuring out how one could best sneak in, stick some fish and slip back out without getting caught.

For the record, I haven't poached or trespassed since I was a foolish boy, but I find an odd sort of comfort in the idea that I haven't forgotten how to do it. On that stretch of the Frying Pan it would be easy. Anyplace that makes such things could copy that big, campaign-sized button you have to pin on your vest. There are enough landowners involved that anyone who saw you would assume you were a guest of someone else. You'd fish out in the open, standing erect, and wave happily at anyone who happened to pass by. By the time they realized their mistake, you'd be long gone. You could probably only get away with it once, but if you were doing it just to prove a point, once would be enough.

But, as I said, I'm not a poacher. These are just entertaining mind games in the same league with, say, sexual fantasies.

I can't tell you exactly where the embarrassment I feel on private water comes from, but it's real enough that it comes from somewhere. Maybe it's because I spent so many years gazing longingly at private water I thought I'd never get on and alternately hating and envying the people I saw fishing there. I was doing that in my twenties when, typically, one's sense of idealism takes shape. As you grow older you get either more realistic or more cynical (two shades of the same color), but that perfection you once saw sometimes comes back to haunt you.

I know it's not a perfect world, but if it was there'd be enough good water for everyone and all of it would be public; open to the mob, that is, because the water and the fish would be considered the property only of God and the People. If the fishing wasn't good for everyone who wanted to wet a line, then the fishing would not be considered good for anyone.

But of course the mob wouldn't *be* a mob, they'd be a loose society of sporting ladies and gentlemen, each with good manners and the environmental conscience of a saint, so there'd be no vandalism, no garbage and only the occasional fish kept as needed for food.

Naturally, there would be lots of water and so few people (courteous people, at that) that crowds would never be a problem.

In this Utopia there might not be such a thing as money, but even if there was, it wouldn't be used to buy privilege or to close land and water, so there'd be no hard feelings, no class warfare.

Where was I? Oh yeah, back in the real world where the number of anglers is growing while the amount of fishable public water shrinks, and where, just that year, I'd fished a private trout club in Colorado, some private bass tanks in south Texas, private spring creeks in Montana, a private salmon river in Scotland and so on. After all, as I keep telling myself, it's my job.

Okay, but then I know how my luck runs. Anytime I start thinking I'm actually getting close to some kind of inside track, something happens to remind me that I am, as always, just another guy standing on a stranger's front porch with his hat in his hand.

My friend Jack called me once and said he'd wangled permission to fish a spring creek that he (and the precious few others who have fished it) tell me is easily the best trout stream in Colorado and probably one of the best in the country. And there's no aesthetic sidestepping here. It's the best, they say, in terms of numbers of large trout that can be caught on dry flies between about mid-April and the end of June, and then again in late summer and fall.

So Jack and I were scheduled to fish this thing, and it

hadn't been an easy matter; at least not for Jack. I was just along for the ride, having done nothing more than pick up my phone when he called.

To get on the stream, you have to not only know the owner but also somehow get on his good side, which I'm told isn't a snap and can't be done with money. Then you have to negotiate with the old guy who sold the place to the current owner a few years ago, but who still lives there raising his horses, caretaking the stream and, of course, fishing.

The old man is in his eighties and, like all old cowboys, he is bent, gnarled and gimpy from being kicked by and thrown off of large animals all his life, but I'm told he's still a great fly caster.

We were supposed to fish there on Thursday, but we stopped in Wednesday just to say hello to the old man and let him know we were in the area.

"How's the stream look?" Jack asked.

"Not good," the old man said.

He told us the flow was down and he was afraid his fish might be getting stressed. He wasn't sure we should fish it.

We all went over to have a look at the stream, and Jack and I both thought it had a good head of water in it. There were five or six trout rising in the first pool we came to, and at least two of them looked very large.

I said, "It doesn't look bad to me," and the old man said, "Yeah, now that I look at it, I guess it'll be okay."

"Okay," Jack said, "we'll see you in the morning."

That was about one o'clock in the afternoon, and we spent the rest of the day fishing another nearby creek that was also said to be very good. Jack said it was a little low, too—though not dangerously so for the fish.

The famous Mother's Day caddis hatch we'd hoped to

hit wasn't quite on yet (there were a few caddis flies in the air, but no rising fish), so we worked weighted nymphs in some of the deeper holes.

It was the kind of fishing I say I like best: dramatic and a little bit painstaking, so that every fish caught stands out as its own small victory. We worked the stream for about five hours, and I landed four trout. The smallest was 19 inches.

The next morning we drove back to the fabled creek where, Jack said, I should be ready to achieve Nirvana. "Even on a mediocre day," he said, "it's like nothing you've ever seen before."

We were putting on our waders in the driveway when the old man hobbled out. He said that the owner had come by yesterday to look at the stream and had decided it was in fact too low and we shouldn't fish it. Sorry.

Jack, who is well known for his wisecracks, was speechless. I, just along for the ride, as I said, was now just along for the ride home.

That's how it is with private water. You fish—or not —at the whim of the owner, and I accept that because somewhere in my straight line of radical populist leanings there's a snarl of respect for private land. It would have been nice if the guy had changed his mind before we made the five-hour drive and stayed overnight, but those, as they say, are the breaks.

I guess I was a little pissed when we were turned away, but by the time I was driving up the last stretch of highway toward home I'd convinced myself it was probably for the best. I mean, if I fished the finest trout stream in Colorado now, everything else would be downhill, and I'm too young for that.

Does that sound a little hollow? Well, so be it. That's my story and I'm sticking to it.

●

Not long after that, A.K. and I were doing a book signing at a fly shop in Denver. A young guy came in, bought a book and said he was taking the whole summer off to fly fish before he went back to school to do some graduate work.

He was clean cut and well dressed, so I took a wild guess and said, "Law school, right?"

He said, "Uh, well, yeah," looking around a little guiltily.

I said, "Don't worry about it. In ten years you'll own a nice little spring creek somewhere and A.K. and I will be knocking on your door asking to fish it."

He smiled. He probably thought I was kidding.

That was all last season. This year, Steve and Larry and I suddenly have a little piece of private water of our own. It's a small bass and bluegill pond, and it doesn't seem very elitist to us if only because it was a gift. One day the woman who owns it said casually, "You know, if you guys want to stock and manage my pond, you can have it to fish in." No lease, no money changing hands, no strings, just the rare logic of generosity: I own a little pond, I know some fishermen who seem like nice enough guys, why not put the two together?

This is a plain, small stock pond, just big enough to be more than a puddle, just deep enough for fish to winter over, with year-round water from a spring, a small island and cattails on the uphill bank. It's not beautiful, but it's handsome in a homespun, practical way, and it's a ten-minute drive from my house, two dirt roads from the highway.

The pond bottom is a little on the featureless side, so the first thing we did was make five big bundles of brush to sink at the deep end for cover. Then we stocked it with 8-inch bass and lots of fathead minnows. At this writing we're in the process of transplanting crawdads, frogs and a variety of warm-water insect nymphs from surrounding ponds and lakes. We want as natural a fishery as we can get while still stocking three thousand fatheads as fish food.

For a while we considered getting a shipment of hybrid bluegills from a hatchery in Georgia—a kind of designer panfish with a high growth rate that don't over-populate and stunt because they're sterile—but in the end we decided on plain old, garden-variety, sexually active sunfish.

The pond will take a few seasons to develop, but in time it should be okay and it *could* be great. The hardest part will be not fishing it for a while so the fish can settle in and start to grow up.

Once the woman who owns it said she thought it was kind of sad that these fish only existed to be caught. I said, "Look, it's also kind of sad that as far as the government is concerned, *we* only exist to fight the wars, pay the taxes and believe the lies." I'm sure that made her feel better. Anyway, she never mentioned it again.

We will take our friends to the pond once it's up and running—we've already agreed on that—and I think we'll be generous about who our friends are, but even if the woman who owns the place would stand for it, we won't put up a sign reading, BASS POND—OPEN TO THE PUBLIC—EVERYONE WELCOME.

The pond won't have to be posted because it's out of sight of the road, and the driveway, though long, clearly *is* a driveway, complete with mailbox. There's usually someone around, and if not, anyone who just wandered in there would have to deal with Khan.

Khan (or Khan the Magnificent, as I like to think of him) is a large, black, impressive Great Dane. He was taken in a few years ago as a sick, hungry stray, and the theory is he was mistreated as a pup, because he doesn't like men.

The first time we all went out to the pond, it took Khan about ten minutes to decide to let us out of the car, and then there was a moment when we didn't think he'd let us back in.

A few days later we came back with the five bundles of brush, a box of large-size Milk Bone dog biscuits and Steve's young son, Julian. It's men Khan doesn't care for. Children and women are okay. So while Steve, Larry and I tied up the bundles with nylon cord and weighted them with rocks, Julian fed Khan the whole box of treats.

Since all dogs are basically whores, the deal was struck. Now when we drive up to the pond and Khan comes roaring out like the Hound of the Baskervilles, all we have to do is roll the window down a crack and slip him a Milk Bone. You can almost see the light go on as he remembers: Oh yeah, I don't like men *in general*, but I'll make an exception for men with dog biscuits. So Khan is now our buddy, proving once again that everyone has his price.

11

Blue-winged Olives

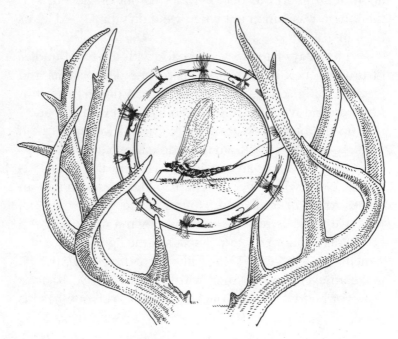

*T*here are some things in life that seem unfair. Don't worry, I won't go down the entire list, but consider that here in Colorado deer season comes right in the middle of the best Blue-winged Olive mayfly hatch of the year. Some friends and I usually hunt deer in the second of the three regular rifle seasons, the long one during which the weather almost always turns wonderfully wet and cold.

There's good tracking snow then, but it's also classic Blue-winged Olive weather.

For the last few years we've hunted up in the headwaters of one of the state's best trout streams. In the tailwater stretch down below the dam that week, the #18 Olives are boiling out of the riffles, big rainbow and brown trout are eating them, and the colder and wetter it is, the better the fishing gets. I wouldn't say the trout are exactly easy even on the best days, but they feed well and you can catch them.

This is the latest predictable hatch on this river and some people fish it, but the weather is often foul, so most of the fair-weather fly fishers are gone, and many of those who also go after deer, elk and/or grouse are out hunting. The crowd that remains is relatively small and it's comprised of the kind of people you don't mind running into on the water, even if there are still a few more of them than you'd like.

In other words, it's just about perfect, and this is all happening forty-five minutes downstream by pickup truck from the cabin we hunt out of.

The first year we hunted up there, I took along the fly-fishing gear. You know what I was thinking: I'll bag my deer in the first day or two of the season and then fish for a week while the venison hangs out in the shed to age properly. It'll be the cosmic cast and blast trip: big fat mule deer, big fat trout on dry flies, a warm cabin with a fireplace and a bed with sheets to come back to at night, and no telephone.

Well, there actually *is* a phone within walking distance of the cabin, but I don't tell people about it. This is one of those rare situations where you can control reality. Just say, "I can't be reached," and sure enough, you can't be reached.

So that first season I packed the fishing stuff: vest, waders, every fly I owned in size 16 or smaller, plus a fly-tying kit in case two hundred-some flies wasn't enough, and three or four light fly rods. As A.K. says, "You pack the rod you're going to use, plus a couple of others you *won't* use."

I had a spare rifle, too, and lots of ammunition—the one bullet I'd use, plus a couple more boxes. I try to pack sensibly and efficiently for trips, but somehow my pickup always looks like I'm off to spend a couple of years explor-ing a new continent.

Most years, A.K. goes fishing during that middle deer season. He approves of hunting—any professional fly tier who buys bucktails by the crate would have to—but he doesn't do it anymore. Maybe he would if the timing of the season wasn't so inconvenient for a dry-fly fisherman. When we both get back there's the usual comparison of notes. He'll say, "Well, did you get your deer?" and I'll say, "Yeah, did you get your trout?"

Then he'll tell me all about it. The hatch he fished was invariably the best he's ever seen—the longest with the most bugs and the biggest trout—the implication being that every year I miss it, it gets a little better.

The autumn Blue-winged Olive hatch can be a long one around here, so I do get to fish it a few times before deer season and at least once or twice afterwards on a couple of different rivers. But, according to A.K., the abso-lute, orgasmic height of it comes during that one week to ten days when I'm out in the woods with the .30-06.

I've often thought of compiling a Plain English/Mess-ing With Your Head dictionary as a public service. It should be written down somewhere that "We're sorry" really means "Actually, we're not sorry at all," that "To help us serve you better . . ." translates as "Pay us and then do the work yourself," and that "The fishing was the best I've ever seen" only means "You weren't there."

The Blue-winged Olive is my favorite mayfly if only because I've fished the hatch so often and for so long. I think it was the first mayfly I identified (or had identified for me) and I know it was the first dry-fly pattern I got into after deciding that maybe a guy should have something besides an Adams in five sizes.

These bugs are found on almost all of the streams I fish in Colorado—not to mention some more exotic spots —and they're multibrooded, so there's usually both a spring and a fall emergence. The autumn hatch always seems better to me, but that may just be because it's more poignant: the last of the mayflies, then midges and then winter. Around home the Olive hatches give things a nice, cyclical flavor, and stumbling on the flies *away* from home makes something click so hard it's almost a physical sensation. I think, Okay, I'm probably gonna catch some trout now.

And there's also a feeling of permanence to it. I've caught trout on Blue-winged Olive hatches in psychological conditions ranging from cocksure insolence to emotional wreckage; through two wives, a number of girlfriends, several presidential administrations, dozens of jobs and hundreds of crises that seemed absolutely pivotal at the time, but most of which I can barely remember now. Life hurtles forward, but in an unsure world that one mayfly hatch is as familiar as my own eye color or shoe size.

A.K. and I have come close to blows a couple of times over the exact color of this fly, as well as, in a more general sense, whether or not getting the color perfectly right helps you catch more fish. I say copying the shade of grayish olive *precisely* isn't necessary, but I do use A.K.'s carefully worked-out colors now on the premise that if it doesn't matter, it can't hurt, either—and I suppose, to avoid having to listen to the lecture again on those days when he catches more fish than I do.

I carry lots of flies for the Olive hatch: two or three nymphs, a couple of emergers and no less than four patterns for the dun. My best is a parachute with a dyed quill body and split hen-hackle wings: a slightly fancier variation of A.K.'s good old Olive Dun. It's a killer, but it takes a little longer to tie than most and it's not all that durable, so I usually save the pattern for tough trout in slow water.

I also carry the spinners: #18 and #20 Red Quill and chocolate-colored dubbed body jobs, some with feather wings and some with poly yarn. Most of the entomologists say the Blue-winged Olive spinner isn't important, which is true most of the time. But then every few years there's that hour and a half when it *is* important. It's not the few extra trout that makes tying the flies worth the trouble, it's that feeling of being deeply hip.

There are fishermen around—the few true experts— who understand lots of different hatches on lots of rivers. I've always wondered how it would feel to reek of wisdom like that, and I think I can get an inkling of it with the Blue-winged Olives. I probably don't know as much as I think I do, but, if nothing else, I have this profound feeling of recognition. When the flies are on the water, I honestly know what to do, and then what to do if that doesn't work and so on. I can also watch the weather at certain times of year, decide that the hatch must be coming off on a river a hundred miles from home, drive down there, and sometimes it is. When it isn't, I can only assume the bugs are sick.

So I brought along the fishing stuff that first season we hunted deer high up on the famous trout stream, and it was something of a disaster. The first day I hunted quickly and impatiently, which of course is insane, because deer hunting is one of those endeavors where hurrying is worse than useless. Over the next few days I managed to slow down to something like the proper pace, but I was still anxious and distracted. I knew the deer would be up on the ridges, but I kept finding myself down along the river. It does hold some trout, but up that high at that time of year you won't see them rising. I looked anyway.

One day I decided the hunting was bad and I should just go catch some trout, but by the time I'd walked back to the cabin I realized the hunting wasn't bad, I was just hunting badly, so I went back out. Poor state of mind. Running in circles, literally and figuratively. Unable to focus on the here and now because of . . . Well, there's no other word for it but greed. I wanted it all so badly I wasn't gonna get anything.

I felt a little better the next day when one of the guys in the party actually walked over to the phone and checked in with his office. The rest of us talked about throwing him out, but it was his cabin.

To make a long story short, I never got fishing and I didn't get a deer. When I got home I called A.K., who'd spent several days on the South Platte River that week.

"How was the Olive hatch?" I asked.

"Oh God," A.K. said, "you shoulda seen it!"

(I thought, Yeah, as it turned out, I shoulda.)

Then he asked, "Did you get your deer?"

"Uh, no, not this year."

"Too bad," he said.

The lesson here was one of those complicated ones involving things like respect for the game, inner peace, avarice and concentration. The fact is, we modern Americans seldom get it right. We live entirely too well in some ways and not nearly well enough in others. We either want more than we need or settle for less than we deserve, and we never seem to understand what we're doing wrong at the time.

Last year I must have done it right. In the two weeks before deer season I fished the Blue-winged Olives half a dozen times, mostly with A.K. The fishing was great, and at least one of those days was what you'd have to call perfect: cloudy, cool, lots of bugs and more big trout than anyone has a right to expect. You know, one of those rare times when you walk away from rising fish, thinking, How many do you have to catch before you've proved your point?

Then I went deer hunting and, on the third day, made a shot comparable to the longest, prettiest cast you ever pulled off. There was that inevitable moment of sadness and elation, and then the hard work, but I thought, this is a better reason than most to not go fishing. I hadn't brought so much as a single fly rod, so after that I spent some time looking for blue grouse and helping haul out two more deer.

Later in the week I even spent an hour or so sitting on a stump with the shotgun in my lap, mulling over nothing in particular. The deer season isn't the last event of the year or anything, but it's still the kind of milestone that should be observed by a good hour of stump sitting. I remember thinking, There's still a lot to do, but there doesn't seem to be anything to do *right now*.

When I got back I called A.K.

"Get your deer?" he asked.

"Yeah," I said. "How was the hatch?"

"Oh, man," he said. "It was amazing. I mean, it was . . . "

"Tell the truth," I said, "was it better than that day two weeks ago, you know, when I caught the big rainbow and then the big brown on the next cast and you were so busy catching fish you didn't even want to take pictures?"

"Well," he said, "I don't know if it was *better*, but it was that good."

12

The Buck

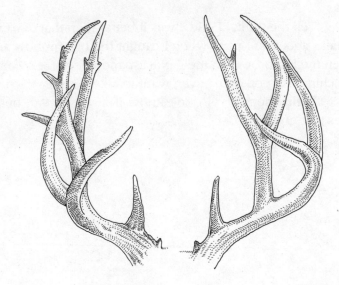

*B*efore last deer season, I'd have told you I haven't cared much about antlers for the last ten or fifteen years. I don't mean I'm not impressed by a great rack or by the hunting skill it often takes to collect one, it's just that in recent seasons I've evolved into a meat hunter and, as every doe stalker has said at least once in his life, you can't eat horns.

This isn't a big philosophical position or anything, it's just the way I've come to think about it. I can't say I hunt for food alone, but I also won't kill something I'm not going to eat, and that has slowly and steadily led me away from trophies—or at least I thought it had.

This last season, Ed, DeWitt Daggett and I hunted the same rugged piece of national forest on Colorado's West Slope that we've been going to for a number of years now. It's a great place: There's game in the woods, but not enough to qualify it as one of the state's more fashionable big-game units, and large parts of it are either too steep, too rocky or too littered with deadfall to get around in easily. Consequently, the area isn't usually crowded and it *is* usually undersubscribed, which means that if you apply for a drawing license, you'll almost surely get it.

And we have the use of a neat little cabin over there, too, complete with a fireplace, easy chairs, warm, dry beds and, of course, some huge local antlers from the old days mounted on the wall. It's nothing fancy, but after a day in the woods it seems downright luxurious and the whole setup just couldn't be better.

We'd all drawn the same tags for the rifle season in late October, licenses that allow you to take either a buck or a doe in the first three days of the season, or just a doe thereafter. It's sort of a weird arrangement—but one the Wildlife Commission apparently thinks is for the best—and for a hunter like me it amounts to a regular old doe tag.

Now this turned out to be a year when there were fewer deer around than in recent seasons. The official explanation was that Colorado had had five unusually mild winters, during which the deer herds grew large, followed by a more or less normal one that pared down the populations in some areas. It wasn't a catastrophe—in fact, it's how the population cycle works—it's just that we'd gotten spoiled, and now things were a little more normal than we were used to.

Anyway, we hunted hard on opening day—each of us going to places where we'd done well in years past—without seeing any deer or even all that much in the way of sign. But we didn't lose heart, and I guess that's one of the reasons I get along with these guys so well: We all want success, but we also believe that you have to go where the hunt takes you and accept whatever lessons it offers.

I mean, if you're paying attention, it's actually possible to learn more by *not* getting a deer than by, say, shooting one in the first hour of legal light on opening day, as I did the season before. The only things I learned from that were how to accept dumb luck gracefully and how to kill a week in deer camp.

So we began to study the maps, pack bigger lunches and range into places we'd never gone before, which meant longer, steeper walks and the likelihood of gut-busting drags if we got something, but okay, fair enough.

On the morning of the fourth day I was on top of a high, steep, quartzite ridge. I'd hunted around the base of this thing for the last few years but had never before thought of climbing it. Or, rather, I'd thought of it, but I hadn't considered actually *doing* it. There's a difference.

DeWitt had been up there the day before and had seen what he excitedly described as an enormous buck with possibly the biggest rack he'd ever seen on a mule deer. The buck was already bounding when DeWitt saw it, and although he got a pretty good look at it, he didn't feel he had a makeable shot, so he didn't fire.

Of course the little three-day buck season was over

when I started up there, but I figured if there was a buck there might also be some does, and anyway, the approaching likelihood of getting skunked gave me whatever it was I needed to grunt up there. I don't think it was desperation exactly, more like the resolve to give it a good, honest try so that if in the end I really didn't get one I could feel okay about it.

It was a long, hard, uphill slog, but it didn't hurt quite as much as I thought it would, which was a nice little surprise. And it was beautiful up there. This is a long, Roman-nose-shaped ridge that runs east and west and falls off to the north—into the valley carved by one of the state's best trout streams—in a series of forested benches, punctuated by two sheer rock cliffs and a ragged scree slope. Real geologic poetry. It's mostly scattered pine and spruce near the top, shading into patches of aspen down the slope a ways. There's lots of deadfall and virtually nothing you could call level ground. The woods there had the feel of a place where humans seldom go, although I can't swear that's true.

Anyway, there was a lot of deer sign up there compared to the places I'd been hunting for the last few days. There were fresh tracks and droppings and recently used beds, as well as a whole system of wide, apparently heavily used game trails.

I worked my way on up the ridge until I came to a little saddle that separated the formation I was on from a longer ridge pointing up toward the Continental Divide. DeWitt had described this the night before after he calmed down about the big buck. He'd come in from the other side —a longer route than the one I'd used, but no easier—and he said he was glad he'd made the hike, because it put the topography of the area together for him in a new way. For me, too. From his description, I knew that if I kept on heading west along that spine, things would begin to look familiar inside of 2 miles.

I hadn't exactly hunted on the way up, I'd just walked, trying to make the best time I could. I think that was the correct tactic, because the wind was at my back and no amount of stealth could do anything about the stink of human wafting out in front of me. And anyway, what I really wanted to hunt were those benches, so I went out the ridge, dropped down the north slope a little and hunted back with the wind in my face.

I thought I was still hunting well—stepping slowly and quietly, stopping every few paces to pick the woods apart piece by piece—but then I flushed a doe that had been lying on a bed no more than 30 or 40 yards in front of me. We danced around in some thick brush for a few minutes, but she evaporated before I could get a shot.

I felt bad because I'd blundered into what could have been an easy standing shot. Then I felt good because I'd gotten so close before the doe heard me and because I'd finally seen a deer after three days of hunting. (I'd had a raghorn bull elk in range the day before, but I didn't have an elk license.) I sat on a log long enough to calm down and eat a few handfuls of trail mix, and then hunted on out along the benches.

About a half mile farther on, as I was working my way down toward a narrow bench, I spotted the cream-colored butt of a deer lying on the far side of a couple of young pines. This time the animal hadn't seen or heard me. It was curled up asleep in the pine duff, so I couldn't see its head.

I began working around above the animal, hoping to see the head (and hoping it was a big doe) but I didn't get more than a dozen agonizingly careful steps before I realized I could easily blow this by being too eager. I could almost hear my father saying, in his most impatient tone of voice, "Goddamn it, a good hunter is *patient.*"

So I sat down where I was, with a good view of the deer's back and chest, but with its reclining head behind a tangle of brush, and waited. How long I waited I couldn't say. It seemed like an hour, so it was probably less than fifteen minutes.

During that time, I'd slowly raised the rifle twice to look at the deer through the scope, trying to get a peek at its head; and the third time I did that there was a ripple of muscle along the back and, sure enough, the head came up, along with a huge set of antlers that I think I'd been seeing all along but had mistaken for part of a dead tree.

At first—sitting there waiting—I'd thought the deer looked too big, but then I decided it was closer than I'd thought it was. That wouldn't be unusual, since I've never been good at judging ranges, even close ones. But now I understood what I was looking at: easily the biggest buck mule deer I'd ever seen, probably 300 pounds, maybe more. The side of the rack I could see clearly had five points, heavy prongs, and the beams at the skull looked as big around as my wrists.

I know, in a story like this it's supposed to be the biggest buck the writer ever saw, but this one really was, honest.

He was, in a word, magnificent, a trophy for sure, maybe even one for the books and, now that I had the perspective in hand, a clear, easy shot at maybe 70 or 80 yards. He didn't seem especially alert and he was looking off down the slope away from me, so I don't think he knew I was there. I believe he'd just awakened naturally from his nap.

I wish I could say there was a moment of moral confusion, but in fact the plan came to me easily and in one seamless piece. All I had to do was punch my license for the day before, when the buck season was still on. It would be an entirely plausible story that I'd shot the buck late yesterday when it was still legal, left it hanging overnight and was only now getting it out. The day was chilly and threatening snow. By the time I got Ed and DeWitt and we'd dragged the carcass out, it would have cooled convincingly. My partners would know what I'd done, but otherwise it was the perfect crime.

It's interesting how badly I wanted that buck, being, after all, a guy who claims not to care much about antlers.

I had the rifle to my shoulder already, and the crosshairs just naturally placed themselves on the heart/lung shot. I'd been sitting there quietly long enough for my breathing to be normal and for my heart rate to have slowed some. I clicked off the safety. The rifle felt alive and friendly, the way a rifle feels the instant before a flawless shot, and I had sin and larceny in my heart.

But of course if I had shot, you wouldn't be reading this, would you? I held the crosshairs on until they started to wobble, then I lowered the rifle, shouted something obscene and watched the buck spring to its feet and thunder off down the slope. When DeWitt was describing this animal—it had to be the same one—he said he thought he felt the ground shake as it bounded off. I had assumed he was using a little poetic license, but then I thought I felt it, too.

I stood up, took a few steps, slipped on a teetery rock and fell down hard, bruising a knee slightly and putting an inch-long gash in the stock of my rifle that I suppose will always remind me of that buck. I don't know if my legs were shaky from adrenaline or just from sitting so long in the cold.

Since then I've occasionally wondered why I didn't shoot. It doesn't haunt me or anything, it's just something I think about every once in a while. It would be nice to say I knew I'd never be able to look at those antlers without feeling a stab of guilt, or that I didn't want to involve my two old friends in a dirty little secret, or that I just knew it was wrong and instinctively did the right thing. Or maybe I just suspected that I hadn't quite thought of everything and that I'd end up getting caught. I don't remember any of that running through my mind at the crucial moment though, so I guess I'll never know for sure.

Then again, maybe what I should be wondering about is why I almost *did* shoot.

That night I told Ed and DeWitt the whole sordid story. They sympathized, said they understood the temptation, but they didn't come right out and say they'd have come as close as I did to actually doing the deed. In fact, I thought Ed gave me sort of a funny look, as if, after all these years, he realized he didn't know me quite as well as he thought he did.

They also didn't point out the obvious: that in a normal deer season you're likely to get that one opportunity that fits your skills and limitations like a glove. If you make the shot, that's your deer; if you don't make it, that *would have been* your deer. And when it was the buck of a lifetime and you're not much of a buck hunter, the karmic implications are staggering.

"Well, anyway," I said, "I know where I'm going next year on opening day."

DeWitt said, "Yeah," then thought a minute and added, "you know, the time is gonna come when we're too old to run up hills like that anymore."

"Sure," I said, "but as long as we can, I think we should keep running up there, right?"

13

Carp

I do fly fish for carp and I'm not here to apologize for it, which is how a lot of these stories begin. (That there *have* been other stories should tell you something, but never mind about that.)

I will admit that the first carp I caught on a fly rod was an accident and that, after I saw it and realized it wasn't an enormous largemouth bass, I was pretty disappointed and even a little hesitant to touch the thing. And when I first stumbled upon a couple of local fly fishers who were actually catching carp on purpose, I thought it was either a joke or maybe another little campaign in the sport's ongoing class wars.

But either way, I figured I'd better try it, and when I did, the most natural thing in the world happened: My aesthetics adjusted themselves to fit the situation. I mean, the fish were big (a 5-pound carp is nothing special), they were spooky and sometimes discriminating, the fishing itself was visual and stealthy and I couldn't catch them at first, even though a carp-fishing dentist I know had given me the dressing for his secret, killer carp fly.

Beyond that fly pattern, advice was hard to come by. There was no hot young carp guide down at the local fly shop, no standard carp-fly selection in any tackle catalog and no book entitled *Selective Carp*.

I guess that was the most exciting part: So few people fly fish for carp that very little is known about the sport. If you want to learn how to do it, you have to pick the brain of one of the rare people who's into it, or just go out cold and try it for yourself. In *Carp in North America,* published by the American Fisheries Society, Ronald J. Spitler says, "When it comes to fly-fishing [for carp] we are drifting a bit into the unknown . . ." I don't know about you, but I kind of like the sound of that.

Where I've fished for them the most—in the warm-water ponds and reservoirs of northeastern Colorado—you can usually find carp tailing like bonefish in the shallow flats on hot summer days. They're beautifully camouflaged against the silty bottom, but you can pick them out by the faint, lazy puffs of mud they blow through their gills as they suck in food, or by their tails waving slowly under the surface like big brown flowers. In deeper water you can sometimes locate them by the trails of tiny bubbles they leave while feeding. (I once asked a carp fisher what exactly caused those bubbles, but he didn't know. Apparently, further study of carp physiology and pond bottom ecology is needed.)

Anyway, then it's a matter of casting a weighted fly ahead of a fish, letting it sink to the bottom and retrieving it in front of him, slowly or briskly, depending on his mood. I'm told it's just like fishing crab flies for bonefish, right down to sounding a lot easier than it really is.

Sometimes you'll spot pods of four or five carp slowly cruising off the bottom in clear water. They're as easy to spook as brown trout would be in the same situation, but if you cast quietly and far enough ahead of them, one may peel off and take a slowly sinking or gently retrieved nymph.

And, naturally, rising carp will take dry flies. By the way, a carp rising to insects or whatever floating on the surface is said to be "clooping."

When it comes to choosing fly patterns, the boilerplate logic of fly-fishing works as well as anything. That is, the more convoluted logic and poetry you can cram into it the better, but unless you have a better idea, just copy the food organism.

Carp feed mostly on aquatic and terrestrial insects, crustaceans, crawdads and such—pretty much what trout would eat in the same water. For tailing carp, I've had my best luck with size 8 or 10, drab-colored, weighted flies tied upside down so that their hooks ride up. This keeps you from fouling on the bottom and, since the fish comes at the fly from above, you want the hook on top anyway— a nice coincidence.

One of my favorites is the Tarcher Nymph, invented as a trout fly by Ken Iwamasa of Boulder, Colorado. Tom Austin, lately of Austin, Texas, does well with bonefish flies like Crazy Charlies and Epoxy flies ("Carp don't know there ain't no crabs and shrimp in here," he once told me), and

Steve has come up with a neat little Clouser Minnow variation he calls a Bloodshot Charlie—one of only three or four
patterns I know of that are tied especially for carp.

The carp I've caught, and seen caught, on dry flies ate
trout patterns that more or less copied what was on the
water: grasshoppers, mayfly spinners and so on. Then
again, the first carp I ever hooked on a dry fly took a #14
Royal Wulff, even though he seemed to be eating cottonwood seeds.

I didn't know about it then, but one of the carp patterns I've run across *is* a cottonwood seed. Another is a
deer-hair mulberry. Like the man said, "we are drifting a bit
into the unknown."

I guess I didn't do this entirely for its own sake right at first.
In the beginning, it was just a hoot to do something that
some of my colleagues considered beneath their dignity,
although, to be fair, few of my real friends worry much
about dignity, and most of them who aren't into carp re-
spond the way A.K. does. "I think a guy should do whatever the hell he wants," he once told me.

"Do you want to go carp fishing tomorrow?" I asked.

"No."

Okay, but then, when I couldn't catch one right away,
hooking a carp fairly on a fly became a mildly interesting
problem. Then I caught a little one, weighing maybe 3 or 4
pounds, and it nearly took me into the backing on a 6-
weight bamboo rod and put a set in one of the tips. When
I took the tip over to Mike Clark's rod shop to have it
straightened, he asked, "How'd you do this?"

"On a big brown trout," I said.

"Bullshit," he said. "You did this on a carp,
didn't you?"

•

It turns out that as a fly rod game fish, the average carp is far bigger than the average bass or trout and more widely distributed than both put together. He can be difficult to hook, and he'll usually fight with great strength. In the best carp water you stand a better than even chance of hooking and landing a 10-pound or bigger fish and, since most American fishermen (and especially fly fishermen) don't much like carp, you'll probably have the best water all to yourself.

You know how other fishermen sometimes casually drift over in your direction when they see you catching fish? They do that when you're catching carp, too, but when they see what you're into, they just drift away again. I wish I could make them do that with trout.

Oddly enough, America is one of the few places where carp are generally disliked. In Europe they're highly regarded as a food and game fish and were once reserved only for royalty. In China and Japan they are traditional symbols of strength and nobility. Poets write about them, painters paint them and samurai warriors once rode into battle carrying carp banners.

Carp were introduced to America in the late 1800s to replace some of the native fish populations that we had all but destroyed through pollution, commercial fishing and general habitat destruction. They did well because they were hardy enough to live in the now warm, muddy water that other game fish couldn't handle, and they were well received at first.

But by the early 1900s carp began to fall out of favor as a food fish, probably because Americans didn't understand how to raise them commercially. In Europe, carp for eating were kept in clean, cool water, but here they were farmed in, or caught from, any old hot, murky pond, and they tasted like it.

We eventually came to miss the fish the carp had replaced, but, although it was our fault the water wasn't clear and clean enough for them anymore, we somehow managed to ignore that. According to Rob Buffler and Tom Dickson, in *Fishing for Buffalo,* the American prejudice against carp developed as follows: First we trashed our waters to the point where nothing but carp would survive in them, and then we blamed the carp for trashing the water.

That's unfair, but I guess it's not all bad. The thing I like most about fly fishing for carp is, it's not popular and, with any luck, it never will be. In a way it reminds me of the way fly-fishing itself was way back before it became fashionable. If you were heavily into it, you were considered sort of a nut, and those of us with antisocial tendencies felt pretty comfortable with that. If nothing else, people would leave you alone, and being left alone is one of the great underrated pleasures of life.

Once Steve and I were out in a boat, casting to some big carp that were feeding up against a dam face. A couple of guys wandered out on the walkway above us and watched for a while. Finally one of them called down, trying to be helpful, "Them are carp, you know."

"Yeah, we know," we said in unison.

"Okay," the guy said, and he and his friend walked away.

So, although I've come to think of these critters as big, handsome, graceful, intelligent, wary fish with a kind of quiet, understated classiness about them, they're still "just carp" and most people can't understand why you'd want to catch them. It makes it hard to take all this seriously— and that's how fishing should be. If people don't occasion-

ally walk away from you shaking their heads, you're probably doing something wrong.

In fact, the only fishing contest I've seen that makes any
sense to me is the Big Lip Invitational, fly-fishing's only
carp tournament, held every summer in Fort Smith, Montana. Steve and I have fished in it as a team for two years
now. At first we just saw it as a joke, but after the first one
we began to see it as a more refined, intelligent joke: a
genuine tournament that is, nonetheless, a spoof on tour-
naments.

The saving grace is that there's no prize money. The
winning team (the one that boats the most carp) has their
names engraved on the traveling carp trophy and gets to
bask in ten or fifteen minutes of local glory before the
picnic breaks up and everyone goes home. That's it.

There are also awards for the biggest carp, the carp
with the biggest lips, and a few booby prizes for things like
the carp with the *smallest* lips. The rules themselves are
simple: two-person teams, fly-fishing only, catch and release, no motors, no chumming, carp must have both lips
to qualify.

The field is small—there were sixteen boats in 1993, a
few less in '94—and the entry fee is just enough to cover a
picnic supper and official T-shirts.

Of course Steve and I—not to mention the other Colorado team, Larry and his wife, Donna—have our own T-
shirts. The motto reads, "Carpe Carpio," which we thought
was Latin for "Seize the Carp." We learned later it should
have been "Carpe *Carpium,*" thought about changing it,
then decided that a grammatical error in a dead language
was somehow appropriate for an event like this.

The contest began six years ago as the logical extension of a typical guide's day off. Some of the people who guided trout fishers on the Bighorn River below Yellowtail Dam took to going up above the dam to Bighorn Lake to fly fish for carp on their days off—to relax, to get away from the crowds and to have some yuks. It was fun, it wasn't easy and, guides being guides, some discussions arose as to who was the best carp fisher. Hence the tournament, organized by the Bighorn Trout Shop in Fort Smith.

A few teams from out of state have entered in recent years, but this is still essentially a small, local event held in a sleepy little fishing town in southern Montana—sort of an elaborate guides' day off. It draws no spectators, teams aren't sponsored by tackle manufacturers and this is probably the only thing resembling press coverage you'll see on it. And, although more than one fisherman in Fort Smith or at the nearby Cottonwood Campground will tell you, "We take our carp fishing seriously around here," something in his manner will suggest that isn't completely true.

Considering that the winners of this thing probably qualify as the fly-fishing-for-carp champions of North America, it's all surprisingly casual, although this year we did receive a warning. A guy took us aside and said, "Keep an eye on your boat." It seems that the first year we were newcomers and so had been treated as guests, but by coming back a second time we've become regulars. "Someone could, you know, steal your drain plug or hide your oars," the guy said.

Apparently tricks are played now and then, although it's not always clear what's a practical joke and what's not. On the morning of the last tournament, John Keiser showed up with a primitive-looking carp painted down each side of his drift boat. "Is that a case of vandalism?" I asked. "Oh no," he said proudly, "I did that myself." Someone standing nearby said, "You'll be able to wash that off, won't you?"

Incidentally, hanging on the wall of John's trailer is the only mounted carp I've ever seen in the flesh. It's huge. He says it weighed 20 pounds. Actually, he said, "All I know for sure is, it bottomed out a 15-pound Chitillion scale. Twenty anyway, maybe more."

I don't know if a mount indicates seriousness or not. If I remember right, that was the only stuffed fish in the place, but I guess that's understandable. After all, once you've got a 20-pound carp on the wall, even a 10-pound trout would look puny by comparison.

Steve and I have never won the tournament, but then we've only been in competitive carp fishing for two seasons, so we're still rookies. The first year we were in a three-way tie for second place, which was not a bad showing for a couple of newcomers. Last time we finished farther back, but I caught the biggest carp: a $6\frac{1}{2}$ pounder on a dry fly, for which I was awarded a set of carp notecards.

Still, we plan to keep at it until we can bring the traveling trophy—and the glory—back to Colorado for the winter, although it's always in the back of our minds that no one really cares much one way or the other.

But the best thing about the tournament is the fishing itself. The water in Bighorn Lake is gin clear and cool; the banks are either rubble rock or sheer cliff and there's no bottom feeding, because, at the lower end of the reservoir where the tournament takes place, the bottom is 400 feet down. This is by far the best dry-fly carp water I've ever seen.

The best way to find carp that will take dry flies is to cruise around the shoreline, looking for their snouts quietly poking up through windblown rafts of organic and semi-organic matter where insects, among other things, collect.

This stuff is not exactly classic trout-stream foam and I didn't know what to call it until Steve suggested "schmoots." I like the sound of that and, after all, we do need the terminology. This is a fairly new sport, but it's still fly-fishing, so we have to be able to say things like, "It was a hot, windless afternoon and carp were clooping in the schmoots."

Any bug is fair game for a carp, and matching the hatch does work, but on warm summer days a fair number of grasshoppers get on the water, and Steve and I have found that a small hopper pattern or a light Elk Hair Caddis (either in about a size 12 or 14) is a good bet. The contestants in the Big Lip Invitational are pretty secretive about their fly patterns, so I can't tell you what the real pros use. Last year one guy went so far as to spray paint the lid of his clear plastic fly box so no one could even catch a fleeting glimpse of his carp selection.

Carp feeding on the surface are fairly easy to spot—at least once you know what to look for. The rise is so subtle it usually leaves no ring, even on dead smooth water, and that round, dark nose looks like a waterlogged pinecone bobbing on a gentle swell.

The trick is to put the fly in front of the fish, close enough that he'll see it, but not so close that it will spook him. It takes steady nerves. Carp don't charge the fly, and the actual take is slow and deliberate. The fly disappears, you tighten the line slowly until you feel pressure and *then* set the hook.

The fishing is delicate, demanding and visual, and the carp fight unusually hard in that cool water. Several times now I've been taken well into the backing by carp that weren't all that heavy. Fish over 10 pounds are sometimes landed in the reservoir, but most run around 5 or 6 pounds.

That's not terribly large for carp, but it's bigger than the average trout caught in the Bighorn River.

The local guides have mostly kept this to themselves, but I did hear of at least one party of paying clients who were taken to the reservoir for carp after several good days in a row on the Bighorn. One of these guys hollered, "Whoo, hoo, hoo, hoo!" every time he hooked a carp. He'd done that with trout on the river, too, but up at the reservoir there was no one to hear him so, the guide said, "It wasn't quite as embarrassing."

This last time, Steve and I arrived a couple of days before the tournament and checked into the campground. We planned to spend a day scouting the lake before the contest and maybe a day floating the river for trout. But then after a great day of carping with caddis and hopper patterns, and considering reports that the river was only fishing well with nymphs, we asked ourselves, "Why nymph fish in a crowd when you can catch bigger fish on dry flies in solitude?" and headed back to the lake.

Come to think of it, I never have gotten around to fishing for trout in the Bighorn River. I should do that one of these days. I hear it's actually pretty good.

CHAPTER

14

Travel

*I*f you're a fly fisher, you *will* develop a serious itch
to travel if you haven't already. It comes with the sport: the
nagging certainty that, even if you live five minutes from
one of the best trout streams in the country, the fishing
must be better somewhere else—or if not better, then at
least different in some tantalizing way.

Be prepared to be misunderstood by nonanglers on
this point. Not long ago I went to Labrador with A.K., who
caught, among other things, a $6\frac{1}{2}$-pound brook trout on a
dry fly—a genuine trophy in anyone's book. Not long after
we got back I watched him land a $7\frac{1}{2}$-pound rainbow in a
river just a few hours' drive from home. Sometime later his
wife asked him, "Why did you have to go halfway to the
Arctic Circle when you can catch a bigger fish at home?"

The answer is, "Precisely *because* it's halfway to the Arctic Circle."

Any fly fisher worthy of the name can rattle off a dozen lakes, rivers, streams, keys, coasts and beaver ponds he's heard about and would like to try, places where the fish *may* be bigger than they are back home, and where they're certainly different. The real problem is paring the list down to a manageable size.

The species of fish you have a soft spot for will give you a good general direction here, and in fact many anglers have their own personal "cross the street" analogy to fall back on, as in, "I wouldn't cross the street for lake trout, but I'd go to hell and back for Atlantic salmon."

(For you lake trout fans, that's just an example, okay?)

And I think it's best to forget about what's fashionable this season. If the fish and the location you're interested in aren't splashed all over the current fly-fishing magazines, so much the better. That just means the guides won't be as busy and the waters won't be as crowded.

In my business of writing stories about fishing, it's always tempting to try to sniff out the new hot spots, if only for the scoop, and then frantically bang out the stories before someone beats you to it. But then as an actual fisherman my tactic has usually been to hang back while the jet-set, fun-hog, been-there-done-that contingent invades and pillages a new location. I write and fish because I enjoy both. If I wanted to live a life full of pressure and urgency, I'd get a real job.

I also thoroughly enjoy the kind of country I'm familiar with (after all, it took me long enough to *get* familiar with it) and don't have a taste for the exotic for its own sake. People who do say that travel to strange new places is broadening, and they're absolutely right. I have done some of that and it's been damned educational. You get to see how people do things differently from how you do them and still seem to get along; in fact, they often get along a whole lot better. And you see how Americans are viewed, which, as often as not, is with a combination of amusement and charity.

But there's nothing wrong with intimacy either, and I've noticed that almost all of my travels take me north, through the overlapping ranges of the North American ice-age flora and fauna I know and love: to where there are brown instead of black bears, spruce grouse instead of blues, black spruce trees instead of Engelmann; to where the brook trout, rainbows, cutthroats and such may be bigger, but where they'll often eat the same flies they take back home, cast on the same fly rods.

So far I've resisted saltwater fly-fishing, even though it's become so stylish it's hard to hold up your end of a conversation if you haven't done it. But it can be terribly expensive, I don't have the tackle and my least favorite kind of weather is the hot, humid, oppressive variety.

And then every time I begin to weaken a little, I meet an adrenaline junkie who says, "Once you get one of those silver torpedoes on a fly rod, you'll never want to mess around with trout again," or words to that effect. And I always think, Right, that's just what I need, something to bugger up one of the few remaining loves of my life.

So I usually go north because that's where I usually feel like going. Others hanker to go south, toward the equator, and still others will go anywhere just *because* it's anywhere. That's up to you and it's the easy part. The hard part is choosing a specific destination and deciding on the style and pace of the trip. Sometimes one will pretty much determine the other, but you'll often have the choices of going in cold and figuring it out as you go along; hiring a guide for at least part of the trip; or doing the full-blown week at a fishing lodge.

I've done it all three ways, plus a few ways in between, and they've all had their charms, but be careful of roughing it just to save money. You might find, as I have on occasion, that after driving 600 miles (or flying and then renting a car), plus eating in cafés and sleeping in motels, it wouldn't have cost much more to stay at a lodge. The best reason for roughing it is that you like it that way.

I do like roughing it, and so do most of the friends I travel with. We like the cafés and roadside camps, navigating with maps, changing plans on last-minute whims, stopping at little bait stores to buy nonresident licenses and trying to figure out if the toothless old bird behind the counter is really giving us a good tip or sending us on a snipe hunt. The long, lonely drives are the kind of shared hardships that make you feel like you've really gone someplace and that you are, in fact, a long way from home, being self-sufficient. Even a breakdown in your own pickup truck is more interesting than being stranded in an airport, if only because you can do something about it.

If nothing else, a road trip amounts to several days of running conversation with friends, and since good talk is so hard to come by these days, that in itself is worth the effort.

On the other hand, an arranged trip can have its advantages, too. There's something neat about knowing exactly where you're going, how you're going to get there and how long you'll be staying, having a printed itinerary from a travel agent, being met at the airport by the head guide, having someone else do the cooking. If the camp van breaks down halfway to the lodge, you're still stuck, but figuring out what to do next is someone else's problem.

Barring a catastrophe, all you have to do on a trip like that is fish and ponder whatever comes to mind. Your most momentous decision will be whether you want to go for rainbows again today, or grayling, or maybe try for some char. You can leave your watch in camp and discard your sense of logistics. At lunch the guide will hand you your sandwich, and someone will tell you when it's time to pack up your stuff and go home.

I don't travel or fish to "get away" because my life at home isn't something I need to escape from, but I do find that I think more clearly on a trip. Or maybe "think" isn't the right word. What sometimes happens is, things I've actually given up thinking about just slip into place of their own accord, providing either the answer or, more likely, the realization that an answer is not required.

A couple of seasons ago I was in a Mackenzie boat on the Bow River in Alberta. We'd just drifted around a big, lazy bend, and there was a beautiful gallery grove of mature cottonwoods, lit up by the late afternoon sun, with a flock of twenty or so white pelicans bobbing in the water in the foreground. The guide was pissed at the birds because they scare the trout and he wanted me to fish that backwater, but I thought they were real pretty, and suddenly, out of nowhere, I realized I didn't have as much against computers, virtual reality and all that crap as I thought I did, although that had been the farthest thing from my mind. It began to occur to me that as people spend more and more of their time gazing into boxes with glazed expressions and becoming more and more docile to make things easier for the machines, maybe those of us who are still a little bit self-sufficient will be able to take the world back.

"Goddamn pelicans," the guide said.

I said, "Don't worry about it."

Over the years I've gone on some great trips based on little more than a hunch and maybe a story from someone I thought I could trust, but I've also researched new places in considerable depth, which is easy enough if you're able to talk to strangers on the telephone.

I've called the Division of Wildlife (or whatever they call it) for the state or province I was interested in, then checked with the tourism board, a guides and outfitters association, a couple of chambers of commerce and maybe a few local fly shops for good measure. Then I've topped it off by calling one of the travel agents that deal exclusively in fishing trips to ask, for instance, "Where's the best fly-fishing for grayling in the Northwest Territories?"

Usually, after discarding the claims that sounded too good to be true—and therefore probably were—I've ended up with a short list of guides, outfitters, lodges or whatever.

Speaking of which, you *will* have to sort out some claims. After all, you're now involved in fishing and advertising, two of the three fields of human endeavor where the truth is most likely to be wounded or even killed. (The third, of course, is politics.)

In my experience, hard sells are a bad omen. Remember that good fishing lodges and guide services are among the last businesses that still make it on plain talk, results and a good reputation.

Beware of statements that sound good but also seem to leave something important unsaid, like, "We have a 56-pound salmon mounted on the wall at the lodge" (that was found washed up on the beach, dead of old age, in 1937).

The same goes for photos in the brochure. Okay, the fish is huge, but is the guy holding it wearing spats and standing in front of a Stutz Bearcat?

What you really want to hear about is last season, and if they say, "Well, a guy caught a 12-pound brown trout," your reply should be, "Good for him. How did everyone else do?"

If you encounter too much obfuscation, find another outfit. There are lots of them.

Unless they've been highly recommended by someone you know well, don't patronize a lodge or guide service that can't or won't supply you with references. And *call* the references. It's true that a lodge won't give you the name and phone number of someone who fell in the lake and nearly drowned or who didn't catch any fish because he was in a coma from mosquito bites, but you can still get valuable information, like, "Sure, the fishing is great, but the cabins leak, the food stinks and the guides are surly."

On the other hand, it's possible for the accommodations to be *too* good. You'll run across resorts that can't say enough about their lovely rustic lodge: sumptuous rooms filled with antiques and lavish, gourmet meals. As you'd expect, a place like this will be more expensive, but the fishing may or may not be any better than at the funky, comfortable little joint a mile farther up the same river.

This kind of outfit may even have a different view of fishing than you do. I stayed at a fancy lodge in the Rocky Mountains once, and I knew I was in trouble the first day. The fishing had been slow, but late in the afternoon a hatch of caddis flies came on and some large brown trout began rising. I'd landed a few fish and was tying on a fresh dry fly when my guide said, in an apologetic tone of voice, "Uh, if we leave now we'll just get back in time for cocktails."

We dragged in about ten-thirty that night, having

missed both cocktails and dinner. While the lodge manager
scolded my guide, the chef was roused to make me a cold
sandwich from the leftover venison crown roast

In the end it worked out surprisingly well. I asserted
myself as politely as possible and the staff made allowances
—without grumbling—for a client who actually wanted to
fish.

When it comes right down to it, how posh the lodge
should be is a matter of personal taste and budget, but one
question you must always ask yourself is, Am I going all
that way to fish, or to eat, sleep, have cocktails and look at
antique furniture?

Timing is also important. A lodge or guide service may
operate for six months out of every year, but the fishing
will change drastically during that time. Maybe there's a hot
six weeks in the middle of the season when conditions are
perfect, and then perhaps another couple of weeks right at
the end when the fishing can be absolutely glorious, but
when you also stand a better than even chance of getting
shut down by foul weather. Or something like that. Every
place is different.

If the lodge manager tells you that every single week
of the season is just great, you've either stumbled upon the
cosmic fishing hole or the guy's trying to fill up some mar-
ginal slots.

One sure way to tell when the best weeks are is to see
which ones are already booked by return customers. You
may have to wait an extra season to take advantage of that,
but then fishermen are supposed to be patient, right?

Now I don't mean to give you the wrong idea here.
Most of the professional fly-fishing types I've met are honest, hardworking people who are simply trying to properly

extol the virtues of their lakes and rivers. But, like all fishermen, they remember the good days more vividly than the
poor ones.

Of course there's another side to all this: You have to
tell whoever you're dealing with exactly what you want,
and to do that you must first get that straight in your own
mind. Do you want to fish big rivers from a boat, or small
streams on foot, or lakes, or a little of all three, or don't you
care one way or the other? Do you want to catch lots of
fish or a few trophies? Are you after one particular species
or a grand slam? Do you envision a relaxing trip, or would
you prefer a guide who will either get you into fish or kill
you in the attempt? Do you use dry flies exclusively, or
would you just as soon fish with whatever's working?

I tend to be a dry-fly fisherman myself, and I remember arriving at a remote lodge in western Canada that had
advertised blanket hatches of mayflies and caddis, only to
be told we'd be fishing streamers on sink-tip lines because
the early hatches were over and the late ones wouldn't start
for another six weeks. In the stunned silence that followed
I realized I'd have known that *if I'd only asked*.

That one worked out okay, too. I got an education in
streamer fishing, caught wild Kamloops rainbow trout and
Dolly Vardens, and fell asleep each night to the sighing of
the wind and the giggling of loons. After all, what other
choice did I have?

Still, you want what you want—or at least you think
you do—so don't be shy about calling someone with a list
of reasonable requirements. They're used to it and they
usually appreciate it. They don't want the wrong client any
more than you want the wrong guide.

It's also a good idea to be honest about things like
your physical condition and your skills as a fly fisher. If
you'll be expected to hike 20 miles a day or cast at tourna-

ment ranges into a strong wind, it's best to know that beforehand.

Most lodges and guide services will provide you with a list of things you should bring, usually including recommended fly rod weights, types of line, leaders, fly patterns, waders, clothing and so on. My advice is, bring what they suggest, because you'll probably need it.

Be sure to ask about special baggage restrictions. If you'll be going into a remote area by floatplane or helicopter, expect a weight limit of something like 40 or 50 pounds, which, in fact, should be plenty for most fishing expeditions.

It's almost always best to go as light as possible, and the real trick to packing for a fishing trip isn't so much to bring what you need as to *not* bring what you *don't* need. Most people pack too many clothes. Rather than a complete wardrobe for all the weather conditions you might encounter, try the layered effect with a light canvas shirt and a heavy wool one, plus long johns, sweater, down vest and a good rain slicker: stuff you can wear a few pieces at a time or all at once as needed.

As a chronic overpacker myself, I know it's possible to pare things down nicely by just asking the obvious question about each item you're thinking of taking. For example, "Do I really need this whetstone, or should I just sharpen my knife before I go?"

Different destinations will require at least slightly different gear, but there are four things I always take regardless of what the lodge specifies, all of which, at one time or another, have been worth their weight in gold: a spare rod, spare line, rain gear and bug repellent.

And always bring a nice fat book. In a stormbound lodge many miles from the nearest town, you can either read it or sell it for a hundred dollars.

•

Naturally, some brochures are more helpful than others. For instance, I have some literature from a lodge in British Columbia. It says to bring "a fly box with an assortment of wet and dry flies for rainbow and cutthroat." What? As a veteran fly fisherman, I can tell you there's hardly a fly pattern in existence that hasn't, at one time or another, been used to catch those two species of trout.

This place also lists (in the same almost useless way) suggested tackle for spin fishers. That's another bad sign. There's nothing wrong with spin fishing, it's just that few things are sadder than a sport with a box of dry flies paired with a guide who only knows how to troll hardware. Fly-fishing has never been more popular, and there are plenty of places that specialize in it.

Then there's this other brochure that includes a separate sheet listing specific fly patterns, colors and sizes, broken down into four roughly six-week-long time slots through the season. It's on a separate, photocopied sheet so it can be updated easily.

It doesn't take a genius to spot the more competent outfit.

If the recommendations for gear and tackle in the brochure seem too vague, don't be afraid to call and ask for a clarification. If the clarification seems vague also, consider the possibility that these people don't know what they're talking about.

Finally there's the matter of your own attitude, which can make or break a trip. There are sports out there who seem to think a fishing lodge is a kind of theme park where the rides always leave on time and where Mickey and Goofy will appear on schedule, rain or shine. It's not like that. If it was, it wouldn't be any fun.

The best lodge in the world can only put you on good water with a competent guide in a boat that doesn't leak. The rest is up to you and whatever gods there may be. So you pick the best place you can find in the best area at the best time of year, while bearing in mind that this is real life, and in real life there are days—or even weeks—when the fish just don't bite.

Sometimes things won't be quite as you expected them to be, and if something is either puzzling or clearly unacceptable, you should go ahead and speak up. On the other hand, try to keep an open mind. A friend of mine says, "If a trip was entirely predictable, you wouldn't have to go," and it's not unusual for the most surprising things to be the sweetest. After all, great fishing is like great poetry: It makes the hair stand up on the back of your neck, and if you didn't see it coming, so much the better.

At a remote fishing camp late last season an old friend and I got a guide who scared us a little at first. He looked like an ax murderer who'd slept in his clothes, had hollow-looking, unblinking eyes and he'd mumble a few words only when he thought conversation was absolutely necessary, which in his opinion was almost never.

But after two hours on the water it became obvious that this guy was a Zen master among fishing guides. His battered canoe did precisely what he wanted it to without so much as a lurch or a gurgle from the paddle; he knew where the big trout would be and he knew what they wanted before they did; he could net a fish so deftly it never knew it had been caught; and he could start a one-match fire from wet twigs and brew perfect oolong tea in a used bean can—all pretty much without comment.

We realized we were in the presence of greatness: an authentic, supremely competent backwoodsman of the old school who just happened to be a little on the shy side.

When my friend and I booked another week at the same lodge for this year, we asked for our old guide back.

So my advice is, do the research, ask the questions and in general cover all the bases you can. Then go to a place you've always wanted to see in hopes of maybe having a little adventure there, but try not to be much more specific than that.

And do not, under any circumstances, sit down on the flight home and figure out what the fish cost you per pound.

15

Winter

Winters can be great here in the Rocky Mountains. It's never unrelentingly one way or another, but in a normal year we'll see dank, Midwestern-style cold with sticky wet snow that freezes at night to a crust you can almost, but never quite, walk on; dry, arctic cold with powder that eats snowshoes up to your knees; dark, airport-closing, pipe-splitting blizzards followed by blue stillnesses, which are followed by warm, hurricane-force winds and unexpected thaws that, in turn, are followed by avalanches.

As I write this, it is, in fact, Avalanche Awareness Month here in Colorado.

Naturally there are some thin-skinned types who whine about all this, but most of us just figure they're victimized by deep character flaws that are probably beyond their control. Unless we're cooped up with them for long periods of time, we at least try to be polite.

A good, hard winter bodes well for water in the trout streams the following summer (although a heavier than usual runoff may postpone the trout fishing a little, and there are always those who worry about die-off in the deer and elk herds), but it's also beneficial in its own right. Fresh snow is helpful for tracking rabbits and hares, and it can make pheasants bunch up; the cold freezes the lakes so you can ice fish if you get that desperate for some sport; low, wet clouds can make the late-season geese fly in range and so on.

Things are seldom what we think of as perfect, but they're often just as they should be, and there's almost always some good in that.

I like winter, and this is one point where my girlfriend Susan and I disagree. She's a Spanish/Norwegian hybrid, but the Spanish is dominant, so she doesn't do well in the cold. I'm a German/English mutt—strong on the German —so I do.

Last night at ten o'clock, it was exactly 10 degrees by the thermometer outside the kitchen window, and for some reason I enjoyed the apparent symmetry of that. Susan didn't. I was sitting around in shirtsleeves, drinking something nice and cool, while she was right next to me on the couch, wrapped in a sleeping bag and cuddling a cup of hot tea and a warm cat. She wasn't whining, but she was looking miserable. As I said, it's genetic.

I live in a drafty old house with a woodstove and a weak gas furnace as backup, so you do feel the weather inside. Even *I* won't go barefoot, what with the cold winds that sometimes blow near the floor, but I guess I don't really mind that, even though it's not energy efficient and therefore politically incorrect.

I suppose there are some things I could do to winterize the place a little, but that would seriously cut into the hunting and fishing time—not to mention the fly rod and shotgun budget—and if there's a single thing I've learned in life it's that one must keep one's priorities straight.

I like winter, and I like being out in it hunting, snowshoeing, fly-fishing in the handful of rivers that stay open and even ice fishing now and then. Susan says this is where I begin to flirt with that fine distinction between just being eccentric and being downright nuts.

Granted, it doesn't always *look* like fun to the objective observer. I'll stumble home, beard encrusted with ice, face blue, feet and fingers numb, maybe with a dead rabbit or game bird or some stiff fish, and she'll just shake her head. Don't get me wrong, she loves to eat wild game and is always glad to see it, but when it comes to going out in the cold and wet to get it—and enjoying that—there is no comprehension, no sympathy.

I guess it *is* hard to explain: doubly hard without getting all mystical and macho about it. There's just something about honestly encountering conditions as they are, not beating them, but slipping in neatly and feeling more or less at home. The idea that humans can profit from nature has been a dangerous one for nature, but when the profit is nothing more than a couple of trout, birds or bunnies for dinner and it's garnered on foot, using simple hand tools and weapons, it at least seems honorable.

A few Christmases ago there was a commercial on TV that had me fuming for days after I saw it. A fat woman was complaining about the holidays because there was all this food around and she always gained weight. (The ad itself was for a treadmill, or maybe diet pills.) I guess we're that spoiled now. Half the world is starving, including some of our own citizens, and fat women on the tube are complaining about too much food.

It's possible that the blood sports are largely symbolic now—which is why it's preferable to catch your trout one by one on dry flies rather than to just dump Clorox in the river—but I think it's enlightening to go out and work for some of your food. The pain you feel when the fish won't bite, the pheasants flush a hundred yards in front of the dog or the geese fly out of range of your fowling piece is a reminder of real hunger; not the kind you feel on a post-holiday crash diet, but the kind that comes when there's no damned food.

I got out of my funk by convincing myself, on a pheasant-hunting trip to Nebraska, that the TV lady was, after all, just an actress reading lines for money, which she would use to buy groceries.

It was cold and beautiful in Nebraska, hiking the swales and gullies around the cut corn with Steve and his dog Poudre. It was late in the season, when most hunters had gone home, but the birds were still spooky. We were happy to get a few pheasants and a handful of quail, although if we'd sold them, we wouldn't have made enough to pay for the motel room, let alone meals and shells. Hunting and fishing may be symbolic in some ways, but next to the symbolism of money they look like stark reality.

•

It's almost always beautiful outside in the winter. If you stay away from things like heavily used cross-country ski areas, where herds of sheep in neon clothing congregate, there's a wonderful stillness to things: the Japanese sparseness of a raven perched on a black snag on a snow-covered hillside. It's serene, comforting and always at least a little bit dangerous.

You want to get your share of fish or game and you can't mind a little normal discomfort. On the other hand, you know that, for instance, falling in the lake in shirtsleeves in July is one thing, while going through the ice in four thick layers of clothing in January is another. So beyond the satisfaction of getting where you want to go and collecting some game if you're lucky, there's the added satisfaction of being able to take care of yourself in a situation where some care must be taken.

If you pay attention, you can learn some useful life skills, such as caution, judgment and how to feel confident within your own limitations. At some point—usually after you've already made a few notable mistakes—you no longer have to ponder questions like: Am I a wuss if I go in now, or am I a fool if I stay out? It's like wondering if you should quit drinking: If the question has come up, it means you should.

A few weeks ago, when two friends and I spent nearly all day hunting and I shot the only snowshoe hare, I tried to explain the profound symbolism of it all to Susan.

"The thing is," I said, " 'there will be hunger in the other lodges tonight.' "

"No there won't," she said. "They'll just call out for a pizza."

"Well, I mean, *figuratively.*"

I've noticed that about warm-weather people: Their sense of poetry seizes up at about 40 degrees.

Once she said, "You guys complain about the cold, too, you know. You come home and talk about how awful it was."

"Yeah," I said. "That's part of it: recognizing your human frailty in the face of higher natural powers. I guess it's a man thing."

"Why isn't it a man thing to go to the Bahamas?"

Well, because you don't suffer in the Bahamas, and suffering in the pursuit of sport is meaningful. If nothing else, some modest hardship seems to indicate that there's a little more to this than just dim-witted fun, although how *much* more is a matter of personal choice.

I have friends who feel that hunting, fishing or just trekking in harsh, difficult conditions can lead you directly to the true meaning of existence. And I have other friends who just say, "If you wanna shoot some geese, your feet are probably gonna get a little cold."

I'm afraid I tend toward the more serious side myself, especially in the winter, when even active people spend too much of their indoor time thinking and not enough tying trout flies. The little deaths in sport seem even more real when you hurt a little yourself and when your own core temperature is a bit low. And if it takes all day to get one snowshoe hare—not to mention more burned calories than a 2-pound bunny can replace, even with white wine and sour cream sauce—then that just shows you how things really are: Modern comforts are an illusion; in the real world, subsistence is a full-time job; all food was once alive and so on. Things like hunting and fishing are important because the big, dark hole of mortality is at the center of it all.

See what I mean? Serious.

I enjoy my thoughtful friends—we have some great long talks about this stuff—but in the winter, as I begin to drop into that pensive mood, I think I value those other guys a little more. You know, the ones who hunt and fish for no other reason than that they hunt and fish. The idea of Meaning with a capital *M* is not unknown to these people, they just figure that if it's really there it'll eventually become evident. Meanwhile, one must be concerned with more practical things like warm boots, good gloves, sharp augers, bait and ammunition.

And it's also probably good for me to be with a woman who sees game in terms of wine, warmth and great meals with friends instead of some kind of grim enlightenment. I mean, the big, dark hole is always there, but you don't have to keep staring into it.

CHAPTER

16

Little Flies

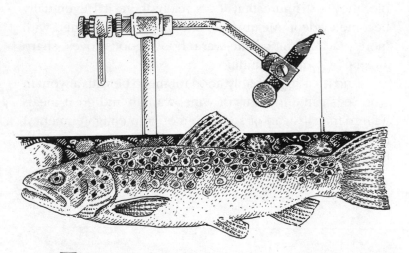

*T*his afternoon I've been casually tying first #22 and then #24 Blue-winged Olive parachutes, working my way down to the #26s. On a good day I actually *can* tie a passable size 26 dry fly, but I have to sort of sneak up on it.

By "casually" I mean I'm stopping now and then to get more coffee, poke the fire in the woodstove (whether it needs poking or not) and stir the pot of slow-simmering game stock: the kind of little rituals that, along with an enforced nonchalance, make me ready to wipe off the drugstore magnifier glasses and calmly tackle an even tinier hook.

Outside, it's snowing steadily; a heavy, wet snow that's more glassy than pure white and that falls straight down like rain, only a little slower. It's classic Blue-winged Olive weather—good for fishing them, maybe even better for staying inside and tying them.

It's a familiar scene, but if I were just dropped here suddenly, I couldn't tell, from either the weather or the flies, if it was late fall or early spring, although what's simmering in the pot might give me a clue. (By spring the wild-game menu has usually come down to the winter's last snowshoe hares.)

On some of my favorite rivers here in Colorado, those two seasons—let's say, roughly, October into November and March into April—are almost mirror images of each other. The weather at either time can be anywhere from comfortably cool and bright to penetratingly chilly with wet nimbostratus clouds lying halfway down the nearby peaks to just plain cold with snow. It's always beautiful, but most days are some kind of struggle.

As far as the hatches go, once the #18 Blue-winged Olives begin to thin out in the fall, the mayflies gradually slip down in size, first to about a size 22, then 24 and finally to some honest 26s, bugs smaller than some of the true midges that start about then and peter off sporadically through the winter.

In early spring it's the other way around. The mayfly hatches sputter along in the tiny sizes for a while—each with its own matching spinner fall—and then gradually swell into the size 18 Baetis again, which by then seems huge.

Well, let's say something like that *usually* happens,

although they'll tell you at any local fly shop that there are no guarantees on fly size or hatch schedule. All trout streams have their moods, and Western tailwaters in the cold months can get pretty spooky.

That's probably why these little mayflies sometimes fall through the cracks of the standard hatch charts into the area of, "Well, you might actually want to have your Blue-winged Olives in 20s and even 22s as well as 18s, just in case," but these days a whole mess of fly fishers are onto them anyway, enough to sometimes mob the water a little at what were once sort of chilly and lonely times of year.

It seems like a lot of people are turning in that direction now: purposefully sniffing out difficult, unpredictable, off-season hatches, not so much to stretch the season as to avoid the crowds. I can remember when you could plan to have the rivers pretty much to yourself between the beginning of duck season and about April or so, but between then and now one of the many changes I've seen in the fly-fishing business is the proliferation of warm, waterproof coats and supposedly miraculous long underwear for foul-weather anglers.

It's still hard to find commercially tied Blue-winged Olives smaller than a size 20 or 22, but maybe that'll come.

Among those who worry about these things, there's some debate over what species these smaller bugs are. I've heard *Pseudocloeons* and *Paraleptophlebias* nominated—and Latin words with lots of syllables do have a nice ring—but unless you're a mad colorist fly tier like A.K., they're just generic Blue-winged Olive Duns in assorted miniature sizes with either pale olive or rusty spinners, which are sometimes on the water at the same time.

There have been times when I've seined the water out

of frustration and found what looks, to the nonscientific
eye, like anything from a two- to a six-part overlapping
multiple hatch/spinner fall. You think these minute differ-
ences in size (and yes, A.K., maybe even color) couldn't
possibly make a difference to the trout, but then if that
were true you'd be catching fish now instead of standing
up to your armpits in 38-degree water, looking at a net full
of bugs.

And on some days, like the one last week when I was
fishing the South Platte River with A.K., Mike Clark and Pat
Leonard, the entire sparse, mixed hatch is channeled down
the narrow, complicated currents along a far, rocky bank;
the water is low and clear; the light is dull, so visibility is
poor; the wind is whipping, so accurate casting is tough;
it's cold, so you're trying to tie #24 flies to 7x tippets with
stinging fingers; and you can stand in one place in the cold
water for so long your feet go numb. You hope they're
frozen, because the only other possibility is that you're
having a stroke.

I don't know why I enjoy this so much. Maybe it's
because I see it as a moral victory for a pampered American
to come to love anything that's excruciatingly difficult and
that doesn't involve money. Or maybe it's just that I spent
a long time thinking this kind of fishing took so much skill
and finesse I'd probably never be able to do it; thinking
that because it's what some people told me, so that, for a
while at least, I was afraid to even try it.

Luckily, I fell in with A.K. while I was still just young
and impressionable enough to learn some new things. I
noticed right off that he'd happily try for fish that seemed
impossible, the same ones I'd pass up, looking for something I thought I could handle. I don't think he felt especially skillful or confident, it's more like he was just curious,
but satisfying that curiosity over and over again had actu-

ally *made* him skillful and confident, whether he realized it or not.

And of course sometimes those fish *were* impossible, but he always figured the worst thing that could happen was, you'd lose your fly, and since he tied flies for a living at the rate of several dozen an hour, that wasn't a catastrophe.

Fishing small flies effectively does take a little doing— or at least some getting used to—but it's not as hard as it's often made out to be. I actually fly fished for quite a while before I realized it was possible to get snookered by certain writers, fly shop clerks and self-styled experts: people who, in order to make money or jump-start their egos, wanted to make this look like only a genius could do it.

But then I began to run into some real experts—you know, people who just knew how to catch fish. They'd show you a little trick here, maybe a new angle there, and say things like, "Just keep foolin' around and you'll get the hang of it."

Twenty-some years later I'm still foolin' around, and I *do* think I'm starting to get the hang of it.

There have been some so-called advances in fly tackle, but it's surprising how little difference most of them make. For instance, tippet material has gotten much stronger in recent years, so where you were once likely to break your light leader on a big fish, you now stand an even chance of bending your hook. There's a book out now with page after page of hook test graphs to illustrate the phenomenon.

Okay, but I guess it doesn't matter to me what breaks first, because either way the fish is lost. What it comes down to is, advances or not, a #24 fly on a 7x tippet is a more delicate rig than, say, a #2 lemming on a 0x. Beyond that, it's just fishing.

•

A.K., Mike, Pat and I all did pretty well the other day on the Platte. That is, we each missed some strikes, broke some fish off and actually landed a few during a sparse, mixed hatch of tiny bugs that lasted, off and on, for a couple of hours.

There have been a few times when I've caught lots of trout on light tackle and tiny flies, but I've learned to count a few fish as a clear success. More than one is always nice, because a single fish could have been an accident, but, if nothing else, a good fishing yarn has some drama in it, and too many fish can make it seem too easy.

Naturally, my best fish was one I *didn't* land. I think it was a brown trout, although I can't be sure. A.K. pointed him out to me, said he'd been casting to him for an hour but couldn't get him to take. Now, a trout A.K. can't catch is a hard one indeed, but as long as you manage not to spook the fish, you have virtually as many tries as you have the patience for, while the trout only has to make one mistake. So, however desperate things look, the odds can still be in your favor.

What you're aiming for is a kind of serene determination. It helps a lot if you just see it as an interesting problem instead of a matter of life and death, and you accomplish that by not counting fish in order to keep score. I guess that's something else I picked up from watching A.K.: I've met a few since, but he was the first fisherman I knew who would really rather catch one difficult fish than ten easy ones.

This trout was rising sporadically in the kind of spot that presents an almost impossible dry-fly drift. There was a cleft in the jumbled, rocky bank that cupped a little eddy where the current piled up, swept backwards upstream and then spilled out into the mainstream again in a lazy, egg-shaped whirlpool.

Even from the best casting position I could get myself into, a good drift to most of it was beyond me, but the trout was moving around in there, and every now and then he'd poke his nose up in a little slip of smooth current on the near side that I *could* get a drift to if I did everything just right.

So I tried something that was either an easy way out or a brilliant tactical maneuver: I just kept putting my size 24 Olive Quill parachute in the one spot where I could get a decent drift, and the fish finally came out and ate it.

I'd thought this was a big trout—which is why I spent so much time on him—but when I set the hook he flashed sideways in the current and I caught a pretty clear glimpse of him. It only lasted a split second, but he looked about the size of the blade on a canoe paddle.

As I said, I think it was a brown, but something about his size canceled out whatever I might have made out of his color.

I'd hooked him along the far bank, and on the first run he blasted downstream and out into the open water of a long glide. If he'd stayed there I'd have had an even chance, but he didn't like it when the bottom started to shallow up on the near side, so he ran back upstream and began boring under the rocks along the far bank.

I felt my leader ticking against the boulders over there, but the light tackle wouldn't let me put on enough pressure to haul him out. I pulled as hard as I thought I could, but it was only a matter of seconds before the fish sawed my tippet in half against the rocks. When I reeled in what was left of my leader, a good foot of it felt like it had been sandpapered.

This was a fish that could have been landed on a #24

hook and 7x if he'd been a little dumber or I'd been a little smarter or the rocks had been a little rounder or whatever, but as it was—in a world where there's still some natural justice—he was one that deserved to get away.

I caught myself laughing out loud about it. A.K. does that a lot, and people have asked me about it:

"How come the guy laughs every time he loses a fish?"

"I guess he's having a good time," I say.

That's a fair question, though, and it took me a while to figure it out myself. At first, quite a few years ago now, I just thought he was nuts. I still think he's nuts, but I've also come to see the logic of it. Fact is, the heartbreaking loss of a great big trout really is kind of funny.

The hooking, playing and losing of that fish probably took less than half a minute and A.K., who was fishing just upstream with his back to me, missed all but the very end of it, when I started giggling. The sound of laughter carries a long way on a trout stream—it's easier to hear than a screaming reel.

He called down to me, glancing over his shoulder, "Did you hook that fish?"

"Yeah, briefly."

"Well, good for you," he said.

17

The Voice

Nick Lyons, the famous fishing writer, editor and publisher, once said, "It's good for the soul to have a closed season," or something very close to that. He was talking about being away from fishing for a few months out of the year so you can calm down, let the past season sink in and

get to all the backup chores, which range from oiling your
reels to pondering the meaning of it all.

He's right, a little distance now and then *is* good for
the soul, but it makes me nervous when that's mandatory.
I prefer things the way they are here in Colorado: The
fishing season never officially closes, so time off is more a
matter of weather and limited possibilities, and if neither of
those things bother you—and your soul seems to be in
decent shape—you can go fishing anyway.

I get more deeply into winter fly-fishing some years
than others. Sometimes I see it as a sport in its own right,
which it is, and other times I just consider it to be symptom-
atic relief from the shack nasties, which is just as true. I
don't know why I go—when I go—but I'm afraid I know
what keeps me from going at times: laziness, complacency,
squeamishness about a little discomfort, all of which I
sometimes try to disguise as "too busy with some very
important projects." Of course that doesn't fool anyone. It's
the rare fisherman who doesn't see through "busy" as an
excuse.

Luckily, this is a cyclical business that seems to affect
my friends and me in the same way, so either a bunch of
us are up for it or none of us are. No explanation there. It's
just that in some mysterious way we share a loose, lead-
erless group consciousness, sort of like a pack of lemmings.

This last winter we got out quite a bit. In January, Mike
Clark and I just decided we had to go fishing and spent a
day up on the Blue River. It was okay. We caught a few
trout, and I lost a hog rainbow—probably a 5 pounder—
because I didn't notice that the line had frozen in my guides
until I got the fish on. There was an instant of elation,
followed by confusion, followed in turn by an overwhelm-
ing helplessness: the kind of thing a fisherman gets used to.

I'm usually only good for one winter trip to the Blue. It's a nice stream with some big trout in it and many miles of water to fish in the summer and fall, but the only stretch of it that fishes well in the winter flows right through the town of Silverthorne, and it's just too strange. The Interstate 70 bridge thunders over the best pool on that upper stretch, and there are places where you'll slog up out of the river to pee and find yourself in a shopping center parking lot.

That makes me sad, because I remember Silverthorne from twenty years ago, before the Interstate came through. Back then it was sleepy, comfortable and not on the way to anywhere. My fondest and most vivid memories are of the bar, but if I remember right, there was also a café, a gas station and a few scattered houses and cabins. This was *only* twenty years ago (or was it twenty-five?) so of course the main form of transportation was the pickup truck, but the bar still had a hitching post out front and you had to be careful not to step in a pile of road apples in the parking lot.

At the time, I was living in the mountains near the town of Montezuma, about a forty-minute drive up a dirt road from Silverthorne. Some friends and I were staying in a cabin up there and working in a struggling silver mine.

It was a classic shoestring operation. The vein of wire silver had run out, leaving behind it a little lead and a little nickel, but the guy who owned the claim was convinced the silver would turn up again if he just kept digging. His investors weren't so sure, so he was reduced to getting a few of us hippies to work for shares and a free cabin to live in. The free cabin was all we ever saw on a regular basis, but it wasn't a bad life. We had good hard work to do, plenty of fresh air (both inside and outside the cabin), peace and quiet, game and fish to eat and a drunken game of pool in Silverthorne now and then.

At that time, Montezuma had five year-round residents. One was the postmaster for life and the other four amounted to the town council. That fall, as I was preparing to head down to civilization for the winter, they told me that if I stayed on till spring it would be my turn to be mayor.

Looking back on it now, I realize this wasn't an honor —all they were trying to do was stick me with some paperwork. Still, it was tempting at the time, but the mine had closed, there was no money, the cabin had been cold and drafty even in summer and, although I didn't know it then, my boss and landlord was only about six months away from getting busted on some kind of investor fraud rap.

I'd been happy living there, but my friends had already left and I knew if I stayed the winter I'd starve, freeze or go insane. So I shot one last game of eight ball in Silverthorne, stepped in something in the parking lot on the way to my truck and drove over to the East Slope, where I arrived with ten bucks in my pocket and horseshit on my boots, looking for work.

I never went back to Montezuma, but I *have* been to Silverthorne and it's become a real dump: rows of factory outlet stores, penal colonies of cheap condos crawling up the slopes, strips of fast food joints manned by surly teenagers—the full catastrophe. The fishing through town is better than ever because of the catch-and-release regulations —and that's good to see, because the fishing usually goes first—but I keep seeing the place through a haze of time and nostalgia, and the whole scene is just too surreal.

Still, Mike and I had gone fishing and caught some fish—even if the ambiance was all wrong—so we were suddenly into the winter program, and over the next couple of months we made regular trips to our old haunts on the South Platte River, sometimes with A.K., Pat and/or Mike Price. The Platte can be crowded—even in winter— and below Cheesman Canyon there's a paved, two-lane county road running next to it, but compared to the Blue at Silverthorne it's like wilderness. Anyway, the ice had been broken and suddenly the whole gang was fishing again.

Now, on any tailwater trout stream in midwinter it's possible to catch no fish or damned few. Typically, you nymph fish steadily all day and, usually sometime in mid- to late afternoon, there's about a forty-minute window during which you catch all your fish for the day. Maybe someone lands as many as three trout and, judging from the other fishermen you've seen and the few you've talked to that day, that probably qualifies him as top rod on the river. On the drive home you gang up on him and tell him being top rod means he has to buy dinner. Now and then it even works.

Except for that forty minutes or so, the river is dead. You don't see many fish, and those few you do see are sitting on the bottom like waterlogged branches, not feeding, not moving, possibly not even entirely conscious.

That happens a lot in the winter, so you learn to fish casually and at a reasonable pace so you're not all burned out and frustrated when something happens—who knows what?—and, for a few minutes at least, the fish bite.

Most days it really does happen. Everyone who has anything resembling the right fly in the water catches a fish or two before it shuts down again. You'll hear theories about why that happens from people who have a pathological need for theories—the most popular one now has to do with drift migration patterns of aquatic insect larvae—but no theory makes it predictable or explains the days when it doesn't happen. In the end, it's a matter of blind faith and a light rod you can cast all day.

Now and then there's a hatch of midges or, rarely, some tiny mayflies, but mostly it's nymph fishing. I almost always fish a brace of nymphs now, and I try to imagine that kind of rig doubling my chances of having the right pattern, but that's not statistics, that's faith again.

On some trips I'll change flies furiously, and on others I'll tie on something that feels right and fish with it all day. It's a matter of mood. Changing flies is something to do, but then searching for the right patterns when the fish aren't biting can seem like nothing but an exercise in knot tying.

And there are lots of flies to pick from: Pheasant Tails, Hare's Ears, RS2s, Miracle Nymphs, Buckskins, Brassies, String Things and a whole mess of patterns that, like the suspects in drive-by shootings, have descriptions but no names, say, a generic black midge pupa with a body of dyed goose biot and stubby gills at the butt made of Hungarian partridge flue. The body of a red midge larva can be made of dyed goose biot, floss, dubbing or wire, and as unlikely as it seems, there are days when the fish will bite one, but not the other three.

In the hope of hooking two or three fish a day on average, there are tiers around here who spend years exploring the permutations of no more than three materials wound on or lashed to a size 20 or smaller hook, either coming up with new patterns or adjusting old ones.

Like the good old Miracle Nymph. It's nothing but a white floss body ribbed with copper wire, but then someone noticed that when the fly gets wet the color of the thread underbody bleeds through a little, giving the thing a barely noticeable gray, olive, yellow or rusty cast. Ed swears this makes a difference. I can't imagine that it does, but when I tie Miracles I faithfully change thread color after every six flies as a kind of observance.

Almost all winter regulars on the Platte eventually fall into this sort of nitpicking program, and we locals like to say that over the years of catch-and-release regulations and matching the hatch, the fishing there has gotten progressively more technical and stylized, although it's never clear whether we're talking about changes in the trout themselves or in the fishermen.

A.K., Mike Clark and I went down to the Platte in early February and had a typical February kind of day. The weather was warm and bright for the time of year (it was the middle of one of our regulation midwinter thaws), the water in the river was low and cold and the wind was howling.

Not the best of conditions—calmer, cooler air, less sunlight and somewhat warmer water would have been much better—but then when you go fly-fishing in winter you keep your expectations reasonable: You'll spend a nice day on the river and maybe you'll even catch a trout or two.

We fished near the little town of Trumbull, and in six or seven hours we managed to land a few trout and hook and lose a few others. All in all, a fairly respectable performance.

When it was all over we had burgers at the Deckers Bar (the only hot food for 30 miles in any direction, but still good) and talked over the day's fishing. We've all fished this river for a long time now, and I said I remembered the winter fishing being a lot better.

A.K. said he remembered that too, but he also remembers that in years past we spent a lot more time down there in January, February and March than we have in recent seasons, and that's important. Much is made about the skill it takes to catch trout on a fly rod, but putting in a lot of time also helps. Winter fishing is unpredictable, but there *are* great days, and the more time you spend on the river, the more likely you are to stumble into one.

And you also have to admit to yourself that memories —especially the good ones—are selective. When I'm casting back ten or fifteen years, I have to remind myself that the days when the trout rose eagerly to dry flies or ate nymphs steadily for three hours straight stand out more clearly than the days when they didn't.

Not long ago I said to Ed that I thought the Platte was getting awfully crowded these days, even in the off-season. Ed's an old South Platte hand and he said he felt that too, but added that, honestly, he thought he *should* be able to remember days when it wasn't crowded, but he's not sure he actually does.

I *can* recall days when I had long stretches of that river all to myself, but Ed is probably right: That was as rare fifteen years ago as it is now.

I guess after a certain age you have to become aware of the dreaded good-old-days syndrome. That comes from having so many recollections stored away that when someone mentions the name of a favorite river you don't do a complete inventory of your memories; you just do a quick edit and come up with something like the South Platte's greatest hits.

After we exhausted the subject of memory, Mike and I

got off on a tangent, giving A.K. some grief because he hadn't been able to go fishing much that winter. He really *had* been too busy, flying around the country to sportsmen's shows to promote his new line of fly-tying tools, but the three of us agreed quite a few years ago now that if any one of us started to take himself seriously, the other two were supposed to straighten him out. I told A.K. that having a corporate address in an eastern city put him on pretty thin ice, but I smiled when I said it so he'd know I didn't really mean it. He told me—also smiling, but not in quite the same way—that he'd be done with the shows by April, at which time he would proceed to fish circles around me.

Fair enough. After all, this happens to all of us from time to time: We actually do get busy with something and miss some fishing. But the trips continue even if you can't go, and you know your friends are out on the water while you're—I shudder to use the word—working, and on the days that doesn't drive you crazy, it's kind of comforting.

By the time the burgers arrived, we'd worn out the subject of being busy and were planning a trip to the Henry's Fork in Idaho for the coming summer.

A.K. and I had pretty much given up on the Henry's Fork after the 1988 season, when drought, low flows, poor management and a few other elements combined to all but wreck the fine old fishery there. In August of 1987 we'd had our best fishing ever on the Fork—enormous rainbows eating dry flies day after day—but in '88 it was so bad we left after two days and ended up on a spring creek a day's drive to the north.

But now the word is the Henry's Fork is coming back nicely. Maybe not quite like the old days, but as I just pointed out, once you get some distance on them, maybe the old days can't really be trusted.

Anyway, it's been seven years now, and we think we should give it another try. Maybe in June for the famous Green Drake mayfly hatch.

True, our friend Mike Lawson (who runs a fly shop on the Henry's Fork) said last year's Green Drake hatch was poor, but then that was last year. When it comes right down to it, there are no guarantees except that every season is a new beginning.

A few weeks later, A.K. was off doing a show somewhere and Mike Clark, Pat and I were back on the river. Once again, it was warm and breezy and the sun was shining: a fine day to be hanging around on a trout stream, but not so good for fishing. Warm days are the most comfortable— and it's a good thing, too, because you'll probably spend a lot of time sitting on convenient logs and having long talks —but the cold, cloudy days fish the best. You know this, but if you get out enough you have the leisure to rediscover it every season.

Thinking back on it, as I'd been doing lately, I could remember my best winter fishing days as agonizing. Numb feet, stinging ears and fingers, the line frozen in the guides and sometimes even on the reel. You can chip ice from the guides—carefully—but if you don't have a fire going, you have to stick the reel in your armpit to thaw it out, which can be really startling. If there *is* a fire, you have to remember that cork grips and reel seats can be singed and plastic fly lines and leaders can melt. That kind of thing.

When you pick a day that's too nice, you gut it out and fish anyway because, assuming you're in the right place and have something like the right flies tied on, there will always be that forty minutes to look forward to. But then off-season fishing is off-season fishing. If the best thing about it is the weather, you might as well enjoy it.

At the right times of year—not to mention certain outstanding but unpredictable days at the *wrong* times of year—the South Platte offers up glorious hatches and many fish. On the slow days you experience something like what invariably happens in a marriage or a long cohabitation: You see your favorite sex object looking decidedly unsexy and, although you do notice, it doesn't seem to make any difference. In the one case, you don't wish for a different woman, and in the other it doesn't occur to you that you shouldn't have gone fishing.

By about three in the afternoon that day, I had wandered away from Mike and Pat and was fishing alone on a piece of water we call The Duck Pond. This is a long, braided run that usually has a lot of trout in it. If there's any feeding going on, the fish will nose up into the head of it. If not, they'll usually fall back to hold in the slower water.

I'd worked the upper end and was slowly fishing my way down the run, being as methodical as possible for that late in the day. I was casting listlessly—doing what I came to do and trying to get used to the idea of getting skunked—when I hooked a fish. It had been so long since I'd had a strike I couldn't recall what to do at first, but I finally got around to setting the hook.

The fish felt okay at first—strong and quick—but after the first run it started to feel both weak and too heavy. Then I saw that it was swimming sideways and I knew it was foul hooked.

I thought, Bummer, the only fish of the day and I didn't get him fairly, so I can't count him. That's crucial, by the way. A fish that's not hooked in the mouth isn't caught fairly and can't be counted, period, no room for discussion. Even a single lapse out of desperation here will start you down the road to becoming a despicable, unprincipled fish hog.

But I'd forgotten that I was fishing a brace of nymphs. When I got the trout to the net and went to unhook him, I found that he had one fly under his pectoral fin and the other in his mouth. Okay, this was a somewhat delicate point, but I figured it was unlikely that he'd gotten foul hooked, then realized he was hungry and eaten the other fly, so he was a fair catch. What a relief.

It was a pretty fish, too—a chunky, beautifully colored brown trout about 15 inches long. I remember thinking, This would be a paltry reward for a whole day's fishing if I was thinking in terms of rewards, and then thinking, What the hell do you mean by *that?* Maybe that it's a lot easier to claim you're not in this just to catch fish after you have, in fact, caught one.

A young guy, maybe eighteen or twenty years old, had watched me land that fish, and after I released it he came over to talk. He asked how the fishing had been, and I said it had been pretty slow. Then he said, a little shyly, I thought, "Well, I'm real new at this, but I haven't caught a fish all day."

I remembered the feeling from when I was just starting out: If you're not catching fish, you automatically assume it's because you're not good enough.

I said, "Well, I'm not new at this at all, and that fish you just saw was my only one today."

"Really?" he asked.

"Yeah, really."

I think that made him feel better, and I felt pretty good too, because I hadn't listened to the voice. You know, the one that whispers in the ear of every fisherman at a time like that, especially on catch-and-release water, where, however many fish you've caught, you won't have any with you: the voice that says, "Go ahead, tell him that last trout makes twenty so far."

CHAPTER

18

Guides

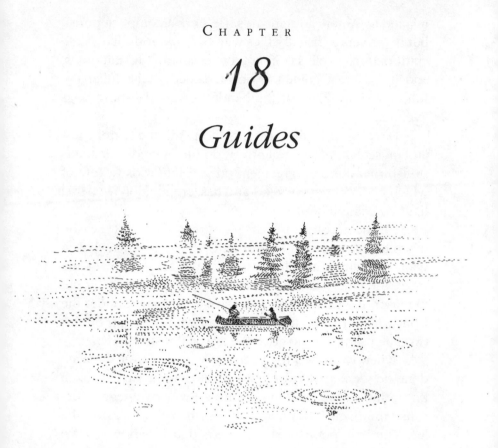

On a recent trip to Alberta, Canada, I did some fishing with Dave Brown and Peter Smallman. These guys are partners—Dave is a guide, while Peter runs the two Smallman's Fly Shops, one in a shopping center in Calgary, the other above an ice-cream parlor in Cochrane. They're the kind of odd couple you sometimes see in the fly-fishing business.

Peter is tall, precise, a little reserved and profoundly

relaxed by American standards. He's not a complete purist, but he prefers to fish dry flies with bamboo rods, likes little cutthroats as well as, if not better than, pig rainbows, and has a great golden retriever named Dame Juliana—Julie for short—one of the handful of good fishing dogs I've met.

Dave, on the other hand, is short with the barrel chest and muscular arms of a big-river, drift-boat guide. He tends to fish nymphs and streamers on graphite rods (a few of which he breaks every year) and has a reputation for being hard core and indestructible.

He demonstrated that indestructibility last season when he managed to run over himself with his own vehicle while launching a drift boat. In the short version of the story, the emergency brake failed as he was stepping out the door, the car lurched and Dave was thrown under the front wheel. He wanted to go ahead with the float, but his two clients insisted he go to the hospital instead.

When we fished together a few weeks after the accident, he seemed okay except for a slight limp on a swollen knee, and he was wading the Bow River bare-legged because the doctor told him to use cold compresses on the leg. The only permanent damage is that he's now known as Dave "Speed Bump" Brown.

Dave and Peter seem to have one of those nearly ideal partnerships. Labor is divided according to temperament, the two of them apparently get along well and, as Dave told me, "If a customer can't relate to one of us, he can probably relate to the other."

Naturally, everyone loves Julie.

Sometimes the best thing about a fishing trip, looking back on it, wasn't so much the good fishing as it was hanging around with the guides. Guides still seem exotic to me, probably because I spent so many years fishing before I ever went out with one. I mean, I was young and poor, with more endurance than sense and more time than money. Guides were a luxury I just couldn't afford.

The good part of that was, I learned how to fly fish in the hit-and-miss, trial-and-error way that makes things stick, and I learned patience, persistence, acceptance and probably a few other good things, too.

The bad part was that, lacking instruction, I developed a few bad habits, some of which I'm struggling with to this day, and I missed out for years on all those neat, practical, all-but-obvious little things a guide can teach you if you just pay attention. In fact, although people have been trying to tell me what to do all my life, the only ones who've been right on anything like a regular basis were fishing guides.

By now I've fished with a fair number of guides and am able to count some among my friends, going back to fish with them again as much for the company as for the fish. Taken together, fishing guides do constitute a distinct breed, but they're not all the same, as some claim. Far from it, in fact.

Many American guides—especially the younger ones —consider themselves to be a combination of teacher, coach, chauffeur, valet, tour director and therapist. They say that's a fairly recent development, caused by the huge number of beginners who are now flocking to the sport.

Once, not all that long ago, a guide could assume that the average client more or less knew how to fly fish, or at least that he could cast a little bit. But now, I'm told, you have to be ready for the sport who has only the vaguest idea of what he's doing, and you have to be prepared to do as much of it for him as possible, while trying to convey the idea that, as long as he's holding the rod, you can't do it all—regardless of how much he's paying you.

And you may also have to patiently explain to him that, although you know the river well enough, you are not actually in control of the fish or the hatches or the flow or the weather or the mosquitos. It's fishing: sometimes it goes well, sometimes it doesn't, and whining isn't gonna help any.

Almost every guide I've ever talked to refers to this as "baby-sitting."

Too much baby-sitting can lead to a kind of smothering, even intrusive style of guiding that makes you feel more like a spectator than a participant, but, to their credit, most of these guys will gladly back off to a polite distance if they can.

On the other hand, I've been with some guides from the old school who figure how good a fisherman you are is your own affair. They'll take you to where the fish are, maybe even point them out to you, but otherwise you're pretty much on your own. If they think you look like you know what you're doing, they'll stand around holding the landing net. If not, they might decide to take a little nap.

I've seen some clients get upset at this, seeing it as either laziness or stupidity, but from the guide's point of view it's the logical course of action. He assumes you're competent—a gesture of respect many Americans no longer recognize—but if it turns out that you came all that way and spent all that money to fish, but you don't know *how* to fish, well, that was your mistake, not his.

And then of course there's the luck of the draw. On another trip to northern Canada, a guide told me, "It never fails. When we have a crappy week, the camp is full of good fishermen. And when the weather's great and there are hatches all over the place, we get guys who can't get their fly out of the damn canoe."

You have to remember that, as a client, you are the raw material, and not even the best guide can make a silk purse out of a sow's ear.

Of course the very best guides I've seen don't *have* a style. They take stock of you within the first half hour on the water and adapt themselves accordingly; either leading you by the hand, leaving you alone or something in between. Somehow they manage to balance the amount of help you want with the amount you need (not always the same thing), and in ways often too subtle to describe, they maneuver you into catching fish you wouldn't have caught without them, but that you nonetheless caught all by yourself.

As you drift along in the Mackenzie boat, your guide suggests that you throw an upstream mend in your cast up along the bank. You can't quite manage it at first, but then your drifts improve as you get the hang of it and you start getting strikes.

But, thinking back on it, did you really get the hang of it, or did the angle of the boat change in such a way that the half-assed mend you were capable of was enough to get the job done?

The guide would probably like you to notice and appreciate something like that, and maybe even reflect that appreciation in your tip at the end of the day, but chances are he'll be too diplomatic to point it out. In fact, if it wasn't for fishing guides, diplomacy could now be a lost art in everyday life.

●

Ed started guiding a few years ago, for a shop down in Colorado Springs, and since then I've noticed a slight change in him. He was always a good fisherman and a courteous and generous partner, but lately he's developed a kind of extra polish.

For one thing, he can now spot fish like an osprey because that's what good guides spend so much of their time doing. Some people think guides are professional fishermen, but they're not. They don't fish; they try to help *other people* fish, which is an entirely different story.

So we'll be walking a bank now, looking for trout on a river we've fished together off and on for twenty years, and I'll say, "There's one."

Ed will look, cock his head a little and say, "Actually, there's six . . . No, seven."

"Huh? Where?"

Maybe it's just my imagination, but he also seems a little more easygoing now, less likely to care if he catches fish, more genuinely pleased if I do, and more likely to do something like fish a dry fly all day because that's what he feels like doing, even if his best shot at actually catching something is with a nymph. Some guides go on automatic pilot whenever they're near water, even on their days off, but most just enjoy the lack of pressure and fish with what looks like a sense of relief.

And now, if I ask Ed what's new, he might say something like, "I had a client last week who'd never fly fished before and I got him into a 23 incher."

It's permissible for the guide to take credit for that, but it's also expected that in another kind of situation he'll say, "Well, there was a nice hatch and I had some good fishermen, so we did pretty good."

I don't mean to say Ed has actually changed. We're still just old friends who travel, camp and fish together in the same old way. It's just that if I went fishing with him now for the first time, I might notice that distinctive humorous, calm detachment and think to ask, "By the way, do you guide?"

On my last day in Alberta, I floated the Bow River with two guides, Mike and Tony, on an unofficial basis—that is, we all fished, and none too hard, either. It was 32 degrees Celsius (about 90 Fahrenheit) and we were fishing dry flies, even though the Bow in summer is known primarily as a nymph river with the chance of an evening hatch.

I've noticed that off-duty guides are often willing to do something like that: I mean, deal with the kind of self-imposed limitation that will probably get you into five or six fish instead of twenty or twenty-five, just out of curiosity.

There was plenty of time to talk, and I heard some good guide stories. Without going into detail, there was the guy who had never fished before but fully expected to catch a hundred trout; the guy who wouldn't listen and never hooked a fish; the guy who whined from dawn till dusk and also never caught a fish; the guy who showed up drunk in the morning and proceeded to get drunker; the guy with the heart condition who kept passing out and so on. Clients from hell: Any professional guide can tell you about dozens of them.

Somewhere during a session like that I always wonder if I've turned up in some guide's stories as the outdoor writer who spent all day getting tangled in his line and breaking flies off in fish. Probably.

Then again, I have to repeat one of the best compliments I ever got. I was sitting around with a guide after a day on the water, and he was talking about different types of clients: intense, laid back, desperate, philosophical, good, bad and indifferent.

"So," I asked, "given the choice, what kind of client would you rather guide?"

"I'd rather guide a guy like you," he said, "but guys like you don't usually *need* to be guided."

What can I say? Fish long enough and you're bound to have that nearly perfect day, complete with a competent witness. Then again, if that guy compared notes with the last guide I was out with, they might conclude that there are two middle-aged, bearded fishermen with the same name.

That day on the Bow River was one of those good days of fishing when damn few fish were caught. We were casting dry flies on a hot, bright day when any fisherman with his wits about him would have been dredging with nymphs, and for me it was the last day of a long, rambling trip that had gone through Wyoming, Montana, Alberta, British Columbia and back to Alberta again. If the truth were told, I was getting a little road burned. About all I was still good for was watching the scenery and missing the odd strike.

Actually, I think Mike said something about that. What was it? Something about how with most clients you have to beat them over the head to get them to look at the scenery. It wasn't a complaint, just an observation from a guy who spends who knows how many days a year guiding. I didn't ask him how many days. Some guides are proud of the number of trips they do in a season, others don't keep track and still others don't like to think about it.

Tony once guided full time, too, but he only does it occasionally now. They say he charges a lot and is able to pick and choose his clients, most of whom are old regulars from way back. And he also gets to do something else every guide would love to do.

"I make 'em a deal," Tony said. "I say 'Look, I can take you to where the fish are and I can tell you what they're biting, but if you can't catch 'em, that's tough shit, ey?' "

19

Game Dinner

I just spent the better part of the morning cleaning up the wreckage from last night's game dinner. This one was built around, but not limited to, a brace of sockeye salmon from Alaska and a big pot of spaghetti sauce made from the last of the venison sausage and hamburger, plus the last of the dried leccinum and boletus mushrooms.

Those two kinds of wild mushrooms should be up about now, so I expect to gather some fresh ones in the next week or so. And of course deer season is coming up. I don't always get a deer, but I always *expect* to.

I suppose there are more elegant occasions for having a game dinner than cleaning out the freezer, but it's become sort of a late summer/early fall tradition around here.

It was a good group: two outdoor writers, one poet, one newspaper editor, an investment banker, a blacksmith, a librarian, a weaver, an environmental consultant, a potter, a bamboo-rod maker and Larry, who is difficult to categorize in a few words.

Naturally, everyone contributed something, from the obligatory bottle of wine to homemade ice cream with fresh wild raspberries to some recently caught rainbow trout that had been lightly smoked but still needed to be broiled.

I always enjoy the casual confusion of game dinners. I'm sort of a flamboyant cook myself (that is, I always take up more room in the kitchen and dirty more dishes than I really need) and then people always show up with things that have to be boiled or broiled or chilled or chopped or warmed up. I have a small kitchen that gets crowded easily, especially with a few bird dogs underfoot.

Last night Ed and Monica had a bunch of mushrooms they'd found that afternoon, which they dumped on the drainboard for inspection, so while I was stirring spaghetti sauce and cutting up salmon fillets, Larry was grilling his trout and Susan was baking her quiches, John Rankin held a seminar on mushroom identification at the sink. As it turned out, there were three varieties, some better than others, but all edible.

Jack was standing at the kitchen window, looking wistfully out at the bird feeders in the backyard and asking me if I'd seen fewer goldfinches than usual this year. He had, and he thought that was ominous.

Molly, the golden retriever, was cuddled up with Donna and the other Susan on the couch. By the look of it, the two women were plotting something, and Molly seemed to be in on it; leaning in, listening closely. Poudre, the Llewellin setter pup, was howling through the screen door at Steve, who was out in the backyard in the rain, grilling the salmon. Poudre hates to be left out of anything even mildly interesting.

I started talking about a recent speech in which a politician had apparently declared a religious war on people like me and just about everyone I know, and I overheard Ed say, "Oh God, don't let him get started on that. Ask him if he's been fishing lately."

Someone in the other room yelled, "So, John, you been fishin'?" I decided to take the hint and said, "Where do you think these salmon came from?"

Sawhorses and a sheet of plywood to serve as a table were being hauled inside because, as I said, it was raining. Rain doesn't *always* change things when you plan to eat outside; last time it didn't start raining until we were on our second cup of coffee. Donna congratulated me on my timing. I said that once you're in tune with the rhythms of the universe, it's easy.

Some game cooks actually plan their meals—this complements this, and both together logically and aesthetically lead to that, all transitions lubricated by the proper wines, of course—but ours are usually pretty haphazard. Someone gets the idea, makes the announcement, and then it all falls together naturally. The theme is wild food, but beyond that it's up for grabs.

Whatever is in season is usually prominent and fresh, but then things come out of half a dozen freezer chests, too, so there's this multiseasonal bounty: trout and rabbit, elk and bluegill, raspberries picked two hours ago and

dried mushrooms from last spring. When you invite someone, they'll ask how many people are coming to determine
how many fish or rabbits to thaw out, but they don't ask
about wine. They know from experience that whatever
they bring will go perfectly with something.

I will say that most of us are good game cooks in one way
or another.

Larry is a master of simplicity: largely plain deer, elk,
trout, bass or whatever, cooked just right, usually over live
coals, with great respect for the meat itself, although lately
he's been learning about sauces.

Ed is an advocate of simplicity and respect to the point
that he believes marinades to be the work of the devil and
will eat any pasta dish so long as it has "those little green
things in it."

I once explained to him, "That's parsley."

"Whatever," he said.

Steve, on the other hand, is a good tinkerer, invent-
ing dressings and sauces with a delicate combination of
thought and bravado. His roast grouse with a glaze made
from boysenberry jam, wine, butter and I don't know what
all else comes to mind. He uses expensive copper pots that
distribute the heat even better than cast iron and knows
about things like braising and poaching.

He's either the best game cook among us or just the
fanciest. When I brought a large grilse back from a recent
salmon-fishing trip, Steve volunteered to cook it. When I
mentioned that to Donna she said, "Yeah, that's my favorite
fish recipe."

"What's that?" I asked.

"You know," she said, "give it to Steve."

Donna is great at combining disparate ingredients into

dishes that make you say, "Jeez, why didn't anyone think of that before?" and at making brilliant minor adjustments. Not long ago she made some mushroom soup with fresh chanterelles and some dried boletes. She ground the dried mushrooms to powder and added that instead of flour to thicken the soup. A seemingly small thing that made a huge difference.

John Rankin knows wild mushrooms frontwards and backwards. He knows what kind of game demands what mycological accent and can make anything from simple battered, fried morels to an elaborate wood-nymph gravy.

My girlfriend Susan cooks instinctively in what I would call the Upper Midwestern school. She pounces on a main ingredient without benefit of a recipe or, apparently, even a clear idea of the finished product, so there's always an element of suspense, although she has risen above the Midwestern tendency to cook food into submission and then crumble potato chips on top of it. She refuses to document her results, so some of her best dishes are now just poignant memories.

I have a handful of specialties—snowshoe hare stew, venison spaghetti sauce, grouse paprika, mustard beer battered fish—the recipes for which I pirated from books or friends and then slowly, over time, changed enough to make them my own.

More than anything, I'm fascinated by the idea that if you shoot a rabbit you can either spend half an hour breading and frying it or you can take all day to make stuffed roast wild hare with Russian game sauce, sending someone else out for the wine because you don't dare leave the kitchen for even ten minutes. It just depends on how you felt when you woke up that morning: like a mountain man or a country gentleman.

I also think it's interesting that a week-long bout of death-grip writer's block can be cured by an experimental wild hare Dijon that turns out even moderately well.

So, is game cookery an art? The long answer begins "define art, define cooking, define game . . ." but the short answer is yes.

If nothing else, most people don't know how to prepare wild game. They treat venison like beef and end up with shoe leather, or they smother snowshoe hare until it becomes unrecognizable. The thing is, game is good. What most people call "that gamey taste" doesn't usually come from the game itself but from improper care.

Getting game takes some skill and knowledge, but apparently more people know how to do that than how to take care of the stuff once they have it. It's something we've lost from buying our food wrapped in plastic, killed for us by someone else. The fact is, if you're not going to clean, skin, cool, age and otherwise care for the meat you hunt, you might as well just scrape up roadkill.

And yes, trout caught on dry flies and rabbits shot with small-bore flintlock rifles *do* taste better.

Every once in a while someone asks me why I hunt and fish. Even when I try to answer that question seriously, I never seem to come up with the same reason twice, which means it's either so simple it should be obvious or it's too complicated to go into. But at least a small part of it has to do with the sense of celebration that settles around eating game.

You feel like you're in elite company. Just the fact that

the food is there means that many of those present have a modicum of native intelligence and the ability to use some simple tools. That can't be said of every dinner gathering.

Of course the trick to a game dinner is to invite the right people. Most of my friends are into hunting, fishing and/or some other kinds of foraging, so we appreciate the quality of the food—which is better than almost anything you can buy—and we also appreciate that knowledge, skill, persistence, patient harmony or some other endangered human trait put it on our table. That's why I like these people so much. As my dad would have said, "They may not be perfect, but they know what's what."

So there's always some praise, maybe even a toast, because shooting a deer or catching a fish really is both more difficult and a lot more satisfying than going down to the store to buy a chicken. Game, fish and other wild edibles are all reminiscent of specific seasons; of knowledgeable, reasonably self-sufficient people roaming the countryside and of freezers filling up and emptying again as the year plays itself out.

It's not a matter of survival anymore; it's more like gourmet subsistence. Most of us couldn't afford to eat this well this often any other way, but we do because we live near open land, and have guns, fly rods, a little free time and the modest gumption it takes to get off our butts and go do something.

As Larry says, "One way to enjoy life is to live simply and elegantly within your means." (The other way is to make a lot of money in such a way that you don't spend too much time at it or end up in jail.)

Eating game also introduces you to the concept of restraint, which in turn raises some interesting questions: How much good food is enough? Is it always proper to kill your limit? How much difference is there between what you want and what you actually need? The answers aren't always immediately evident, but it's something to think about.

And then there's death itself. It's not something you want to dwell on, but it's worth understanding in a casual, everyday way. All food was once alive, and to live you've gotta eat. If there's a larger, darker question in there, it's unanswerable and therefore not worth wasting time on. It's just that all good cooking celebrates the transitory nature of reality. I mean, the morning after the best dinner you ever had, you were hungry again, right?

CHAPTER

20

Spring Creek

As I write this, a few friends and I are planning a small, low-budget tour of some Montana spring creeks. Tentatively planning, that is. Ed is making the arrangements, and I haven't heard from him yet, so it's still up in the air and, in fact, may or may not come off.

We usually think about a spring creek trip every season and then end up actually making one about every second or third year. The problem is, some of the better known spring creeks can be booked up a year or more in advance, and since most of us can't see more than a few months into our futures, we don't always plan far enough ahead. When that happens we're either shut out or faced with going through one of the guide services that buy up blocks of days, and that can get a little steep.

That's not to say the guides aren't worth the money, because most of them are, nor is it to say that any of us couldn't *use* a guide. It's just that the expense can seem a little extravagant.

I guess one of the reasons we get along so well is that, although we all have our private indulgences (ranging from good whiskey to bamboo fly rods) we still tend to be a little tight with the money—even when we have some, which is not all the time, and almost never all at once.

As it is, six days on private spring creeks should run us about $300 apiece in rod fees, but if we sleep in that free campground on the Yellowstone River, cook our own meals and tie most of our own flies, we'll still feel like we're living righteously frugal, bohemian lives.

That's *most* of our own flies. We always drive in to one of the fly shops in Livingston to buy handfuls of the latest spring creek patterns—designed by the spring creek experts—and to get the current hatch reports, which are always a little more detailed after you've dropped some cash. I've noticed that this stings a little less as the years go by, even though the flies I buy are usually patterns I could tie cheaper and almost as well myself. But I guess shelling out $50 a day just to get on the water does sort of lubricate the wallet.

I know, fifty bucks isn't much anymore—it's a new fly line and change, maybe a good (though not great) dinner —but when you've grown used to fishing free public water, paying to get on a trout stream can be something you have to get past.

There's always been a strong populist tradition in American fly-fishing—one I've bought into from the beginning—but there's a parallel history of private waters, exclusive clubs and expensive resorts that goes back just as far, and in darker moments it's possible to imagine that we'll eventually become like Europe, where virtually all the good fishing is not only private but also hideously expensive and portioned out according to class.

Of course class consciousness isn't unheard of in America, but to our credit, we're pretty embarrassed by it.

Not so in other parts of the world, though. If you voice your misgivings about exclusiveness on a salmon beat on a private estate in Scotland, you might hear a guy say, without a hint of irony, "It's not a problem. After all, common people *prefer* rough fish."

You may be either too polite or too stunned to ask, "Then why do you need a full-time water bailiff to chase away the poachers?"

Most of the spring creeks I know of are a long way from that, even though they're private and have been for generations. Here in the West at least, there's something about the hydrogeology of them that causes them to rise in fairly level country near mountains, and they were grabbed up by the early settlers for their good river bottomland and year-round sweet water. I'm told that back then the fishing and duck hunting were secondary considerations.

But now ranching and haying don't always pay the bills—a man once told me the way to retire with a million dollars after a lifetime of ranching was to start with $2 million—and the owners of most private creeks are doing what I think just about anyone would do in the same situation. They're either keeping the fishing to themselves and their friends if they can afford that, or charging for it if they can't.

Putting envy aside, I have to say that doesn't bother me or anyone I know. I'm glad there are some spring creeks you can get on just by paying a fair price (that is, without having to beg or know someone), and frankly, if American fly-fishing does go aristocratic in years to come, it won't be because some ranch families are using rod fees to help pay their taxes.

There. That concludes today's sermon.

Naturally, the good spring creeks are few and far between. The strict definition of a spring creek is one where most of the water comes out of the ground instead of from runoff or snow melt, as in a freestone stream. If there's a good, year-round head of clear water, if the springs are deep enough to maintain a more or less uniform temperature, if the water wells up through limestone to give it the right chemistry and if the banks haven't been stripped and beaten down by cattle, you get what fly fishers think of as an archetypal spring creek: a stream with lush vegetation that supports aquatic insects in the billions and trout that grow big and fat on more food than they could possibly want. But that's a lot of "ifs."

The last time I fished a spring creek I was with Ed and it was early June. That's a good time in Montana because the hatches are on, but they're not in full swing yet and the weather can still be tricky, so a lot of fishermen wait until later in the season. The point is, there might be some open slots, so you can get on even if you haven't planned the trip a year or more in advance.

The way I remember it, when we realized we'd be going through the Paradise Valley anyway, we called pretty much at the last minute and lucked into days on two of the creeks. We called a third, but the woman on the phone laughed and said, "You mean the fifth of June *this year?*"

That was an unusually frantic trip, the kind I've been trying to avoid for the last few years, though not always successfully. I think we did eight streams in nine days— starting with the Boulder and ending on the Firehole—but I'm not completely sure of that, and when I try and call it up, it begins to swim together with other drives through that country. (As a guy said down at the café the other day, "The memory is the first thing to go, and I can't remember what the second thing is.") I know I kept a diary of the trip, but I think I left it in a motel room in Lander, Wyoming, on the way home.

But if a good part of that trip is now lost in the ozone, I still remember the spring creeks pretty clearly. The weather was cool and fitful, with periods of bright sun mixed with clouds and rain squalls. The Pale Morning Duns had begun to come off and the fish were onto them but, as I said, things weren't in full swing yet, so the creeks were almost empty.

Mobs of fly casters aren't a crapshoot on pay-to-fish spring creeks like they are on public water because most creeks only allow a limited number of fishermen per day. Still, these are small, intimate streams, and when they're booked full they can still seem a little too crowded.

I think I actually prefer spring creeks before every-thing really gets going. The relative lack of other fishermen is nice, and although those roaring hatches where the may-flies get behind your sunglasses and up your nose are fun, sometimes they're harder to fish than sparser, slower hatches where the fish have fewer bugs to choose from.

Then too, the trout are sometimes a little more eager earlier in the season. Now big, spoiled, catch-and-release

spring creek trout are seldom what you'd call pushovers—
although, like all of us, they do have their stupid moments
—and they never get a real vacation because hard-core
types fish the creeks year-round, sometimes at cheaper
rates in the dead of the off-season. But in late May or early
June the fish haven't been pounded steadily for months on
end and may be a little more likely to rise to a real winged
dry fly instead of some floating nymph or sub-emerger sort
of contraption. That's important to me only because I think
dry flies with wings are pretty.

But spring creeks are famous for snooty trout, and it's
still possible to get into that old routine where the fish are
feeding, but they won't bite, and you're changing from one
pattern to another while fighting off a sense of impending
doom.

At times like that you should avoid thinking that you
paid good money to do this, and if the idea won't go away,
try reminding yourself that you didn't buy fish, you just
rented time on a stream that has fish *in* it.

My standard Montana spring creek Pale Morning Dun is the
one you can buy at any fly shop in the area—a post-wing
thorax tie with split tails and a dubbed yellow body that's
sometimes called a Lawson's Thorax. I also try to have
a split-wing thorax, some goose-shoulder no-hackles and
some parachutes. The Montana patterns are a brighter yellow than the Pale Morning Duns we tie back home in
Colorado (ours usually have a pinkish or rusty cast), and
sometimes changing from one color to another makes a
difference to the fish.

That's eight fly changes, which seems like a lot, but if
none of those work I'll float a standard Hare's Ear or Pheas-

ant Tail nymph, and after the obligatory stop at the fly shop I'll have a bunch of captive, crippled, ruptured and fetal patterns to try.

On a particularly difficult fish, I'll usually only go through two or three fly changes before I start to think maybe it's my drift that's bad. Then I'll try a few short casts for practice, maybe go to a lighter tippet or tie the next fly on with a Duncan loop instead of an improved clinch knot, to let it ride more naturally on the water.

Or maybe I'll change position, moving up- or downstream a little or even crossing to the other side. This takes time because you have to move slowly so as not to disturb the water with too much splashing, but it's often the best way for a mediocre caster to get a better presentation.

I always think the people I'm with are too busy with their own fishing to notice any of this, but then when I run into one of them later they'll almost always ask, smiling, "Well, did you ever catch that one?"

You tell yourself, This is why you wanted to fish a spring creek in the first place, right? People told you they were lousy with trout and bugs, but they were also very difficult to fish, or "highly technical," as some like to say; the kind of water where the really good fly casters come to do their stuff. You wanted to see that and you thought you were up to it.

If you're like most, it doesn't matter if you were up to it the first time or not. If you wired the hatch and caught fish, it was glorious; if you didn't, it was glorious in another way. Novelist Peter Hoeg once said, "When you're young, you think that sex is the culmination of intimacy. Later you discover that it's barely the beginning." Fishing is like that: Even when you catch one, it's barely the beginning.

So you sucked it up and fished a spring creek, and when it was all over you wanted to do it again, either to repeat a performance or to do better next time—and because it was just plain beautiful, as advertised.

It's possible that in true sport there is no failure, only varying degrees of success, and, after all, fishing teaches you to have the courage of your convictions. You wanted it to be tough. It's tough. Okay . . .

If you get skunked on a spring creek, you're in the same boat with some of the world's great fly fishers (whether they'll admit that or not), and if nothing else, a day will come somewhere else when the fishing is pitifully easy: You don't know what to tie on, so you start with a big Royal Wulff and it works; you cast poorly, but trout take the dragging fly anyway; you can't see to land them because of glare or darkness, but they swim into your landing net by themselves.

When that happens—and it will someday—you can think back to that blank day on Armstrong's, Nelson's or DePuy's and think, What the hell, I had this coming. Basically, everything works out well in the end if you just fish enough.

I've fooled with spring creeks off and on for years, and each time I got to fish one it was a treat. By now I guess I can catch trout as often as the next run-of-the-mill fisherman, but I'll never be a hotshot at it because I don't fish spring creeks enough and because I've gotten myself into an awkward bind on that account. That is, I'd somehow like to be as *good* as a hotshot without doing the work or having the competitive nature it takes to actually become one.

As it is, I can fish hard and experiment with patterns

and strategies for a while, but when things really get puzzling my attention sometimes begins to wander. I start trying to identify those warblers in the bankside bushes (even though I have enough trouble with that when I have a bird book and a spotting scope), or I'll find myself pondering one of the abiding mysteries of the universe like, "Why are sock sizes different from shoe sizes?"

That's when I break my own rule, because, after all, the real value of rules is sometimes found in the exceptions. I say to myself, Look, you paid hard-earned cash to be here, so pull yourself together.

21

Desperation Creek

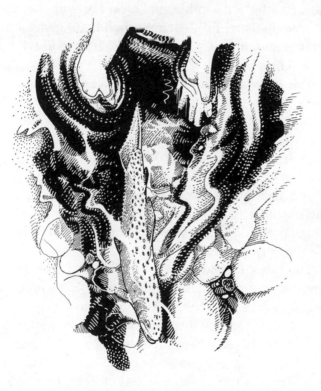

*F*or once I don't have to make up a phony name for the stream I'm talking about because the man who owns a nice long stretch of it has already done that. He calls it "Desperation Creek." Things being as they are, there may actually *be* a Desperation Creek somewhere in the Rocky Mountain West, but of course this isn't it. Or at least not yet. I'm sure the name began as a combination joke and smoke screen, but now the owner uses it with a straight face, which is how real place names evolve.

There's no great story about getting on the stream. I met a man at a party a few years ago, and in the course of things he said if I was ever in the area again I should come by and fish his little spring creek. So last summer when I was back up there, I called and asked if the invitation was still open and, if it was, could it please include Ed, who I was traveling with.

The answer was yes, and that was that: almost too easy to be fun.

Desperation is an archetypal small Western spring creek. Looking out across the meadow from the road, you don't see the stream. If you didn't know it was there, this could just be another several hundred acres of rough pastureland, although it should go without saying that on this stretch at least, no big, stupid, clumsy cows muddy the water or break down the banks. So unless you know better, that's the only clue: no cows.

The creek meanders in its shallow cut through open country where the tallest scrubby bush is no more than waist-high. When I saw it, I thought it was lovely and perfect, but I also thought it would benefit from a little shade. Then I remembered a Xeriscaper telling me how a grove of hundred-year-old cottonwoods could suck a little stream like this dry in the summer. Okay, forget the shade. It's perfect as it is.

Our host assigned each of us half the stream—starting roughly in the middle, Ed worked upstream and I worked down—but first he took us around to show us where the fish were. Some of the spots were obvious, like a deep bend pool with a cut bank, but others were more obscure, the kinds of places where, on strange water, you'd inadvertently spook the fish if you hadn't been warned.

We'd walk from place to place far out away from the creek. Then, coming up on a spot, we'd crouch and finally kneel, and the man would outline the proven approach to each spot: "Stay low from here on down, don't get any closer than that bush and cast from your knees—sidearm." This is a guy who knows his fishing, and I could tell he really hoped we'd do well. (The stream itself is very small, but there are some big trout in it.) He couldn't tell us everything in a few minutes, but he wanted us to fully understand the delicacy of the situation.

Then he wished us luck and left, saying he was too busy to fish. Maybe he was, or maybe he just knew that three people would be one too many. Real generosity isn't always obvious.

Ed and I had been traveling and fishing for at least a few days by then, so we'd worked out most of the kinks. We were as sharp as we get and feeling confident. As we split up, Ed gave me a clenched-fist salute and advised me to "have courage."

I went to the first spot I'd been shown: a gentle riffle with a fair-sized pool below it, where four or five trout were rising. I couldn't see the fish themselves because the light was wrong, and I'm not that good at guessing fish size from rise forms. I crept over to the stream at a shallow, fishless stretch downstream to see if the bugs on the water were really Pale Morning Dun mayflies as I suspected. They were. Good.

Then I crawled up toward the pool, knelt by the bush and began working out line for my first sidearm cast. I hooked a shrub on a back cast and had to crawl back there on my knees to get my dry fly. When I was younger, I used to do this kind of fishing in roofers' knee pads. Now that I —and my knees—are older, I seem happy enough to crawl around unprotected, chewing gravel holes in my waders and sometimes hurting myself. Who knows why? Maybe I finally realized that life is going to cause some damage and there's nothing much I can do about it.

I cast for the bottom trout first. One cast was short, the next not quite so short and the third was pretty much right on. The trout moved 6 or 8 inches and took the fly daintily. When I set the hook, he wiggled once and shot out of the pool toward me. I saw him go by, heading downstream, as I was trying to gather line to take up the slack. It was a rainbow, 20 inches long or more, but by the time I got control of the line he was gone.

There were two more trout still rising in the pool, one about a yard ahead of the other. I neatly hooked and landed them both. The first was about 10 inches long, the second more like 8. I tried to make myself think: Look, they're trout, they're real pretty and you caught 'em. This is great, right? Never mind that you blew the big one.

At the next spot there were two fish rising tight to the far bank, one so close he was making a half-moon–shaped ring, the other maybe a foot out and 2 feet upstream. You naturally assume that the more difficult fish is the biggest, so I got into position and planned a cast that would put the fly almost, but not quite, on the bank, and then let it drift past the first fish and within an inch of the feeding lane of the second one.

It nearly worked. I couldn't have been off by more than a fraction of an inch, but that was enough to stick the fly securely on a wet, rubbery, pencil-sized root. Before I

could think of what to do, the leader bellied heavily in the
current and the two fish stopped rising.

I broke the fly off and then took a few minutes to calm
down and to replace my 6x tippet and size 18 Pale Morning
Dun thorax dry fly. I thought about waiting the fish out,
then realized that the sparse hatch had been on for a while
and wouldn't last forever. So I moved on to the next spot,
where I hooked and landed a nice 14- or 15-inch rainbow
out of a pod of several risers. The fish jumped twice, spook-
ing the rest of the pool.

A little farther downstream I spotted a trout rising near the
bank in a spot I hadn't been shown. It was there that I
started hearing the voices: a man and a woman, clearly
angry, though I couldn't make out what they were saying,
and also the occasional sound of a slamming screen door.
It had to be coming from the little house, half screened by
Russian olive trees, about 200 yards away, just over the
fence line on the next property. I hadn't noticed it before.

I cast from my knees and caught the trout on the third
or fourth drift. It was a chunky, silvery rainbow about a
foot long.

Then, as I was walking on downstream to the next
pool, staying far back from the stream so as not to spook
the fish, the woman's voice carried clearly through the still
air. It said, "You *bastard!*" I could see now that they were
hauling furniture from the house to a pickup parked out
back. I thought, Okay, the main thing here is, this is none
of your business.

I remembered the next pool. It was an L-shaped bend
with a steep bank on the outside and an open gravel bar
on the inside. Kneeling in the grass 30 or 40 yards away, I

could see a few trout rising near the head of it; casual, sporadic dimples. I couldn't recall how my host had told me to approach this one, but it looked as though if I crept up the long leg of the L on the inside, right at the water's edge, I could get to a spot far to the side and a little below the fish. A slight right hook would keep the line out of the gravel, and the back cast looked clear.

I slithered down the bank and began crawling upstream toward the pool. The same openness that would leave plenty of room for a back cast made me feel awfully exposed, so I stayed as low as I could, on my knees and one hand, carrying the rod low, moving with an awkward, hopping limp like a dog with a bad foot.

At about 40 feet the angle of the light changed so I could see the fish. One second the stream was a dull silver sheet and the next the water was clear as air, green bottomed at a depth of roughly 3 feet, with mottled brown rocks. There were only two trout that I could see and they were both huge: easily 20 inches, possibly more. One fish was pale—probably a rainbow—and the other looked very dark, almost black. They seemed to have divided the pool exactly in half, lengthwise, and each one was dancing around in its own half, casually eating mayflies.

From next door, only about 75 yards away now, the man's voice said, "Goddamn it, that's just like you. That's why—" and then the door slammed again.

I crouched there for a few minutes, watching the two fish. Whenever I see game like this—going about their business, unaware that I'm there and that I'm about to catch them or shoot them or (just as likely) do something stupid and scare them away—I often hesitate, savoring it. In some ways, the most beautiful moments in sport are the ones just before you act. You know, open-ended, full of promise, often better than what actually happens in the next few minutes.

Then I cast to the near fish, making a few short false casts first to make sure I'd judged the range and the drift right, and then dropping the fly about 2 feet ahead of him. It was lovely. The fly went past the fish less than a foot to his right. He saw it, turned, followed it downstream and took it gently near the tail of the pool. When I set the hook, the trout shook his head and wallowed on downstream, out of the pool and into a long glide. I didn't want to spook the other fish by standing up, so I followed the run in what must have been a pretty comical knee-walk, but I had just enough time to glance back and see that the other trout was still rising.

I played the fish out in the next pool, far enough downstream that I could lurch to my feet and stand. I suppose you could say it was an unspectacular fight—no blazing runs, no jumps—but when I have a big trout on light tackle, I'm grateful for that. It means I might be able to get him.

When I waded into the water to land the trout, my boots sank in thick mud and a cloud of black muck billowed into the clear stream. My beautiful trout vanished in this crap momentarily, and I experienced panic, but it was okay in the end. The fish was covered with mud, but he was in the net.

I waded out to clear water and washed him off. He was wonderful: as deep-bellied and hump-backed as a little sockeye salmon; olive, purplish red and bluish silver with big spots; 22 inches easy, maybe 23, maybe even . . . Well, I've gotta start carrying a tape measure. Anyway, it was the biggest trout I'd seen in a hell of a long time, and I was real happy.

"You can't take that!" the woman's voice said. "That's *mine!*"

I crawled back up to the pool on knees that felt bruised and that I knew would be sore for days to come, thinking, Hardware store in Bozeman, knee pads, twenty bucks, tops. Sure enough, the other fish was still rising.

When I put the thorax dry fly over him, he executed a heartbreaking refusal rise: He saw it, turned and came for it with his mouth beginning to open and then flashed away at the last minute. It was all I could do not to strike.

The fish ignored two more good drifts with the same fly, so I knew I had to change. For no other reason than that it looked good, I tied on a Harrop's captive dun pattern I'd bought at a local fly shop a few days before. I couldn't see it on the water, but when the fish rose to take something on the surface, I thought it was about where my fly should have been and carefully set the hook.

This trout did exactly what the rainbow had done. He shook his head, ran slowly but heavily down the long run and let himself be played out in the next pool. He was almost an exact copy of the bow: let's say 22 inches, fat and heavy, except he was a lovely brown, the color of burnt butter.

When I released the fish, he cruised to the edge of the main current, belched some mud from his gill covers and then darted under a cut bank. I stood there watching that plume of ugly black muck drifting out of sight around the next bend and wondering how I'd tell Ed about this. Lead up to it? Blurt it out?

I remember my emotions about this being mixed, as they tend to be now that I'm no longer a kid. I was happy about those two big trout, but also vaguely sorry about all the mud I'd stirred up. You can't live without causing some damage, but it occurred to me that maybe over the years I'd caused more than my fair share, although I guess I'd also learned that regret is usually a waste of time. Then again, I knew that when I told Ed the story I'd leave the mud out.

The screen door slammed and the man's voice said, "Aw, fuck you!"

I almost yelled back, "Yeah, well fuck you, too!" but then decided against it. In a situation like that it's best to remain hidden; best for everyone that they never even knew I was there.

What Else Is There?

I used to think I was a fairly radical, not to mention up-to-date environmentalist, but when I look into the newer literature of the movement I realize that I'm not quite an antihumanist anarchist, a primitivist, a humanist eco-anarchist, a green Marxist or an eco-feminist, which are the only choices one recent article on the subject allowed. I probably *am* a bioregionalist (a pretty tame stance these days), but more to the point, I'm a fly fisherman, and that comes with its own political agenda.

My position is, we should have a clean, healthy, diverse natural environment so I can go fishing. Because fishing makes me happy.

Granted, that seems like a simple-minded goal in these grim times, but there it is nonetheless: without becoming overly romantic; without ignoring reality; given the normal limitations; from roughly now until the shit hits the fan, I would like to be, you know, reasonably happy.

And yes, maybe that *is* too much to ask. Then again, I haven't had the dreaded middle-age crisis and I don't detect one brewing. Of course I have an advantage. Half the men and a few of the women I know who've wigged out in their forties wanted to run off and do what I do now, which is fish a lot and write books about it for a living. (The other half wanted more money, faster sports cars and younger lovers, but that's a whole other story.)

These people, after a life of working and striving for money, status, influence or whatever, wanted to chuck it all and become one with nature in some kind of particularly human way, which is the only way available to us. They saw this as a more or less direct route to truth and salvation, and for some of them at least, it was just that.

After twenty-some years of listening to New Age sanctimony, I cringe a little at the mention of becoming *one with* anything, but I guess it's like saying you want happiness: corny but undeniably true.

I started to get into fly-fishing back in the late 1960s, soon after moving to Colorado from the Midwest with no real plans. You could do that back then—live without plans, I mean—and no one thought much of it except maybe your mother.

At first, fly-fishing just seemed like an elegant and practical way to catch trout, and it was also fashionable in a hip sort of way. (Ernest Hemingway fly fished. So did Richard Brautigan. And so, it turns out, does Eric Clapton, as well as a whole bunch of other really cool people who are still with us.) But there was something else, too: It was said fly-fishing was a sport to which one's life could be dedicated.

Okay, presumably that wasn't being said with a completely straight face, but it still had a nice ring to it. I'd been more or less at loose ends since junior high, when it became obvious that if my sister was going to be Queen of the Prom, I was going to be Maynard the beatnik. I guess the idea of dedication didn't interest me much until I realized it could go in some pretty unusual directions.

I'd been fly-fishing for a number of years when, in 1976, an obscure little book called *A River Runs Through It and Other Stories,* by Norman Maclean, appeared from the University of Chicago Press. By then I had it bad, and it didn't surprise me at all to hear Maclean equate fly-fishing with religion. What did surprise me was that some people thought he was kidding.

Robert Redford's movie version of Maclean's story is a good one, much better than most movies made from good literature. They say it did a lot for the sport of fly-fishing, but it also elevated me and many of my contemporaries to instant old-timer status as those who remember when *A River Runs Through It* was "just a book."

Anyway, it was right around then—in the late '70s—that I passed a kind of personal milestone: I quit my job because there was a great Blue-winged Olive mayfly hatch going on and my boss—a man with no soul—wouldn't give me the day off to go fishing. The logic of this seemed flawless at the time, and to be honest, it wasn't much of a job.

Still, it was around then that I decided I'd better become a writer, if only because I wasn't good enough to be a fishing guide or fast enough to be a professional fly tier, and all the other alternatives seemed to involve either not enough fishing or starvation. Luckily, I didn't realize at the time that becoming a freelance writer to *avoid* starvation would not be viewed as the act of a sane man.

So now, because I do write about fishing for a living, I am sometimes interviewed, and a common question is, "What *is* it about fly-fishing, anyway?" Of course the electronic media types who ask this want a cute sound bite before the next commercial instead of the real answer, and once, in an attempt to get into the spirit of the thing, I actually said, "Well, Bob, it's sort of like golf except you can eat the balls." Further proof that writers shouldn't be trusted to think on their feet.

The real truth about fly-fishing is, it is beautiful beyond description in almost every way, and when a certain kind of person is confronted with a certain kind of beauty, they are either saved or ruined for life, or a little of both.

But that's not good enough for most interviewers. "Okay," one radio guy said, "tell me why *I* should take up fly-fishing." (The thing you have to remember is, if you're not recruiting for a cause or pushing a conspiracy theory, you don't belong on the airwaves.)

Not really meaning to be a smart-ass, I said, "Actually, I never said you *should.*"

●

By the time I quit that job to go fishing, I had reached the first plateau. I could cast well enough as long as the situation wasn't too complicated or the range too great, I could locate trout in a stream if they weren't doing something too off the wall, and I could at least guess at what fly to tie on. More to the point, I could sometimes manage to catch a fish.

I caught some that day, in fact—brown trout, two of which I killed and ate for supper—and it's a good thing, too. If I'd gone home that night unemployed and with no fish, I might have become discouraged and ended up in law school.

That was a long time ago, and I still can't claim to be an expert fly fisher, but then I don't have to be. I found that to write about it you simply have to *find* an expert and know what questions to ask, although you do have to fish yourself, if only so you can grasp certain intangibles.

And you don't have to be an expert to see that although what was said about dedicating your life to fly-fishing may not have been meant seriously, it turns out to be true in some extreme cases. And the reasoning is refreshingly simple: Only a few things are worth doing for their own sakes, and life is short.

Just to get good at fly-fishing—that is, to be able to catch fish as often as not in a variety of situations—you have to master the basics of fly casting. That takes a while, especially when you teach yourself, get it all wrong and then have to go back to the beginning and start all over again. In the right hands, fly casting looks graceful and effortless, but when you first try it, you think there must be something wrong with your rod.

Then you have to understand a few things about fish,

the hydrology of the water they live in and the intricacies of fly tackle, while, at the same time, avoiding the obvious pitfall of becoming a boring techno-freak.

Since trout feed mostly on aquatic insects, you have to learn a little bit about the bugs, although exactly how much information you need is a matter of debate. In fact, entomology is where some fly fishers go over the edge, endlessly arguing fine points of taxonomy when all you need is, say, a Pale Morning Dun dry fly tied on a size 22 hook instead of a size 18. At its worst, this can turn fly-fishing into what Charlie Waterman (one of the sages of the sport) has called "a small pool of trout surrounded by a great wall of semantics."

You'll probably decide to tie your own flies anyway, and this will become a much bigger deal than you thought it would.

In the course of all this, you'll learn how barometric pressure, humidity, cloud cover, moon phase, time of day, time of year, stream flow, water temperature and turbidity affect fish and bugs. Or at least you'll begin to think all that means something.

You'll learn how to wade a river and, more importantly, when and where *not* to wade. Slogging through a fast riffle one fine day, you'll suddenly come face to face with the full weight of water, which comes in at 8 pounds per gallon. Drowning is always a possibility, but you'll probably live; most do. If it's a nice warm day you'll dry out in an hour or so.

While others are concerned with more mundane matters, such as who to marry and how to make a living, you'll find yourself pondering questions like: Should my rod be made of fiberglass, graphite, boron or bamboo? Should my line be a double taper, rocket taper, triangle taper, weight forward, sink tip or shooting head? Should my wading shoes have treads, felts or cleats? Should my hooks come from Norway, England or Japan? All of which really can be important—more or less.

You'll surely start reading books and you'll learn all kinds of useful things, but you'll also find that book learning is no substitute for lots and lots of time on the water. There are fishermen who talk a good game but can't catch fish. You don't want to be one of *them*.

You may end up with a trout doormat on the front porch, a trout mailbox, a set of brandy snifters etched with illustrations of trout flies, chamois shirts with embroidered stoneflies over the pockets and a complete set of Susan F. Peterson trout china, but none of that is actually required.

You're supposed to go through a series of transitions. At first you just want a fish, and since this is a complicated sport requiring some skill, landing that first one isn't always a snap. Once you're past that, you'll want lots of fish, then big ones, and then you'll want something like the difficult or the interesting or the beautiful fish, or maybe the fish that swim on the other side of the world.

Finally, you're supposed to see that the real goal of wanting is to stop wanting altogether, so you just go to water out of curiosity and gratefully take whatever it gives you.

It's supposed to be a smooth, straight path to enlightenment—five koans solved and discarded—but I was always a poor student of Zen, the guy who couldn't meditate because he couldn't sit still, so I go back and forth in fits and starts, changing my aesthetics about as often as I change my socks on a fishing trip, that is, every couple of days whether I need to or not.

But if I don't *have* to sit still, I can sometimes manage something that approaches the sublime: that is, just fishing, without the self split in two, with one half casting and the other half watching as if from a distance. It's great. You stare into the water until you realize it's been staring back at you, and maybe you even catch a few trout. But even though I now and then fish brilliantly, I've never quite lost myself as the fisherman and become the fish, let alone become first both and then neither.

But I did come to realize that good fishing and good writing use the same skills. Whether you're after a trout or a story, you won't get far with brute force. You're better off to watch, wait and remain calm, just putting yourself in the place where the thing lives and letting it all happen, rather than trying to *make* it happen.

When a story is going badly, the best thing to do is put it away and go do something else for a while. Maybe go fishing. If the fishing is going badly, the best thing to do is sit on a rock to watch and wait. Sooner or later a crack will open just wide enough to let you slip quietly through. Eventually the story reveals its theme and the fish thinks you went away and starts rising again. The only real skill you've exercised is the ability to stay awake until it happens.

The same strategy has been known to work in politics, business and other more prosaic matters. If you don't know what to do, do nothing for a while. If you don't know what to say, let the other guy talk. Sooner or later he'll let the truth slip simply because he's not smart enough to just shut up. Basically, the world is a big, dumb trout, and you're a fisherman with all the time in the world.

Okay, maybe not. But that's how it seems when you can take things as they come.

Sometimes I wonder what kind of fisherman I'd be if I didn't write about it—or what kind of writer I'd be if I didn't fish—but when it comes right down to it, I can't begin to imagine, and by now it doesn't matter anyway.

In case you haven't noticed, fly-fishing has become fashionable lately. This kind of snuck up on me, so I can't tell you exactly when it happened, but I knew it *had* happened when well-dressed, youngish middle-aged, demographically correct people began to appear on TV casting with fly rods or looking over expensive tackle, not in those insipid Saturday-morning fishing shows, but in slick commercials hawking credit cards and painkillers.

That's how you know something has arrived in America: when they start using it to strike a subliminal chord in advertising.

Some friends and I have occasionally sat down to try to decide if this is a good thing or not, and our consensus is, maybe, maybe not. The only thing we can agree on is, it's startling to be middle-aged and back in style.

Lately, fly-fishing has been described as a "growth industry." (That's supposed to be good news, but it sounds to me like the economic equivalent of cancer.) Stories in the media tell you the newcomers are mostly well-off professional yuppies who can afford the gear and the travel, but then out on the stream you meet old folks and kids, men and women, bums and brain surgeons, polite people and assholes, conservative Republicans and radical antihumanist eco-anarchists. You get along okay with most of them (except the assholes) as long as you don't talk politics.

Some of them are better fly fishers than others, but

their station in life, their income or the amount of money they spent on their tackle seems to have nothing to do with it. In fact, how much they actually know about fly-fishing doesn't always seem to make a difference. This is what Robert Traver meant when he said, "All men are equal before the trout." If he'd written that more recently he'd have said "all persons," which is probably what he meant anyway.

I can't blame anyone for falling in love with fly-fishing, but I have mixed feelings about the growth of the sport. On the one hand, if someone decides to build a dam on a great trout stream, he'll get a lot more letters and phone calls now than he would have ten or twenty years ago. On the other hand, some of those streams are getting pretty crowded these days.

But I'm a conservationist, so, philosophically at least, it doesn't seem unreasonable to trade a little of my solitude for a larger constituency for trout streams. Then again, I've also become a cagey outdoorsman, so I know of some little creeks where I can hike a few extra miles and have my solitude and my trout anyway.

Not long ago Ed told me he thought that small, secluded freestone streams full of small trout were going to be the sport's next rage and that, in fact, some fly shops and guide services were already gearing up for that.

"Oh well," I said, "if worse comes to worst, there's always carp."

As it is now, I can still make those long, brisk walks with a day pack and rod case, unlike some of my contemporaries who have become plump and weary. They make more money than I do, but they spend it on useless shoes and expensive cars that don't even have four-wheel drive.

One of these guys—who also happens to be an old friend—once decided to have one of those helpful, friendly talks with me, just in case there were some larger perspectives on life that I'd overlooked. But it didn't go the way he thought it would and he ended up exasperated, saying, "Jeez, man, *it's only fishing!*"

To which I had to say, "Exactly! And in your case, *it's only the stock market.*" Again, not really meaning to be a smart-ass, but since that's how it came out, okay.

It was a slightly hot moment, but in the end we remained friends. He fishes now and then himself, and sees the value in a simple, healthy life, while I am not entirely opposed to money. I mean, money buys fly rods and plane tickets, right?

And, after all, we're both adults, which, come to think of it, had something to do with his point in the first place. At least he didn't tell me to grow up and get married and get a haircut and buy a Weed Whacker. He just thought that at my age I should buckle down a little, get some equity, think about the future.

Hell, I've thought about the future. I long ago realized that there won't be enough time to fish all the great rivers of even just North America, let alone the world, and that *is* sort of a bleak thought.

On the other hand, it's comforting to think that, even now, there's more good water than a guy can fish well in a lifetime, and although I'm not a kid anymore, I've noticed that I fish better now that I'm older.

It's part of the myth—or at least the accepted pose—that you're supposed to love fishing with a manic, self-destructive craziness. I guess I did once, but I found it hard to locate the stillness I was after while bolting breakfast before dawn with the guides standing around tapping their feet and pointedly looking at their watches. Of course the best guides I know don't even *wear* watches.

There was a time— back before it was a cliché—when I might have said, "No pain, no gain." Now I'd be more likely to say something like, "No patience, no peace of mind," although I *might* just be smart enough to say nothing at all.

I've also noticed that I'm getting more and more reclusive as I try to keep my own fly-fishing from turning from a sport into a business. (Not that it's an endless struggle or anything, it's just something I think I should keep an eye on.)

And I don't mean to say there's anything inherently wrong with the tackle business, either. It's just that you must be very protective of the one or two things you do for love instead of money. I mean, those are the things that give you a vantage point from which to view the rest of the world—or is it a pair of rose-colored glasses?

Anyway, I pretty much stay away from banquets, meetings and fishing contests (except for the carp tournament), and I stopped going to sportsmen's shows not long after I stumbled upon the portable, indoor trout stream at Currigan Hall in Denver a few years ago.

But I still keep meeting kindred spirits. At a party, a woman says to me, "Well, my *husband* fishes! He wishes he could just *live* on the river!" The husband is right there, bourbon and water in hand, and one glance into his eyes tells me this is true. In fact, he wishes he was living on the river at that very moment.

This is one reason why fishermen seldom laugh at fishing jokes: If they hit the mark at all (which is rare), they're too true to be funny—like the bumper sticker that says, SO MANY FISH, SO LITTLE TIME.

There does seem to be an element of desperation about it now and then, but it's a desperation that gets resolved. Fishing is the part of life that's filled with more or less regular successes, and failures that don't really matter because there'll always be a next time. You come to see that a life frittered away with sport and travel makes perfect sense, but no one trip ever tells the whole story.

So basically, I wake up one morning to find that life is strange but simple, and fly-fishing is still as important to me as it was a few decades ago, even though I still can't tell you exactly why, and even though I'm glad it's no more important than it is. It just turns out to be the one part of my life where things are right, or where it seems worth the trouble to try to *make* them right, or maybe the only place where the possibility of rightness even exists. Something like that.

I still can't tell you why I do it. I've tried that a few times and always gotten tangled up in too much sentiment or politics and ended up completely missing the point without actually saying anything I didn't mean. I've read books by fine writers who've tried to explain it. Many failed, and the best only gave tantalizing hints. Jim Harrison said, "Few of us shoot ourselves during an evening hatch." Tom McGuane said, "If the trout are lost, smash the state." Harry Middleton said he's addicted "not so much to fly-fishing but to what it sinks me in."

I think it's now more a matter of unspoken agreements among friends than pounds of fish, and that's probably why I spend more time hanging out with fishermen, as opposed to whoever all those other people are.

Among those others are some well-meaning types who don't enjoy life nearly as much as I do, but who nonetheless believe I should do things differently. They seem to think I'm a decent fly fisher and—a little bit of a temper notwithstanding—a nice enough guy, but that otherwise I'll probably never amount to anything. To that I have to ask, "What else is there to amount to?"